annie sloan's
COLOR SCHEMES

annie sloan's
COLOR SCHEMES
FOR EVERY ROOM

LAUREL
GLEN
San Diego, California

Laurel Glen Publishing
An imprint of the Advantage Publishers Group
5880 Oberlin Drive, San Diego, CA 92121-4794
www.advantagebooksonline.com

ISBN 1-57145-761-5
Library of Congress Cataloging-in-Publication Data
available upon request.

Printed in Italy
1 2 3 4 5   06 05 04 03 02

Concept and original styling by **Luise Roberts**
Project Editor **Jane Ellis**
Designer **Ruth Hope**
Indexer **Isobel McLean**

Contents

How to use this book

This book is about how to use color in your home.

The introductory section explains the characteristics of different colors and how to combine them effectively. The main part of the book is divided into two sections: schemes based on simple colors (which are clean, clear, upbeat), and schemes based on complex colors (which are sophisticated, subtle, contemplative). There are thirty-one decorating themes, ranging from elegant classical to vibrant Latin, arranged from the palest to the

Each color scheme is illustrated with a photograph.

Each title evokes a different mood, which is reflected in the colors used.

Specially created panels graphically illustrate the effect of using the same color palette in differing proportions.

The numbers indicate the complete palette used for this theme.

Cross references to other similar themes.

Rock and Roll

These are the colors of the 1950s, the dawn of a new era that emerged from the war with a new exuberance and irreverence. The colors are bright, uncompromising, unsophisticated primaries and secondaries—sometimes sharp and shockingly fluorescent, sometimes sweet and pastel, but always uncomplicated. This is a palette that is deliberately simple and loud, full of bright colors 'straight from the bottle,' a release from the restricted palette of the war years. Shocking pinks, pale sweet pinks, sky blues, lemon yellows, lime greens, and lipstick reds are the trademark colors of the time. These are counterbalanced with white, black, and gray to create a clean, upbeat, and optimistic look. Black is favored as a trim for almost any color.

A cool kitchen with items from the 1950s and 1960s uses spearmint green and brilliant yellow. Simple materials, including glass and vinyl, and plastic finishes complete the theme.

See also
Candy Jar,
Glam Diva,
Rococo.

Rock and Roll
1-6

1 Sharp Lemon

2 Orange Zing

3 Sputnik Red

4 Neon Blue

5 Baby Blue

6 Shocking Pink

simple colors

Numbers on the palettes help you to relate each color given to its swatch featured on the right-hand pages.

brightest within the two sections. Each theme uses a palette of colors shown as swatches to suggest ten color schemes.

The color schemes are shown as slabs of color, roughly proportional to the amount that should be used in the room.

The colors can be used not just in paints for walls, ceilings, woodwork, or furniture, but also in wallpaper, fabric, carpet, or other materials. For example, look from above and visualize a carpet or rug and a sofa with pillows. Look again and imagine a wall with curtains, an armchair, and a door. The metallic colors represent gold frames, metallic accessories, and light fixtures. If you find a color scheme you like but one of the colors looks too dark when placed on another, white can be added to it without changing the color.

Using photography, the second spread on each theme illustrates the same palette in different proportions and style.

A separate panel of swatches to show colors that have been lightened by adding white.

Numbered swatches relate to both the palettes shown on the pages and to the recipes given on pages 154–158.

This room displays
an understanding of
color. Though many
colors are used
together, the effect is
successful because of
the tonal values of
the colors.

Training your eye

Learning to combine colors skillfully will ensure that your decorating schemes enhance your rooms and suit your preferences. As well as studying the effects produced by different color combinations, you can train your eye by comparing subtly different tones of a particular hue to see which colors combine to make it.

Theoretically, all colors can be mixed from just three primary colors—red, yellow, and blue—plus white. Mixing any two of these in equal amounts produces a secondary color: red and yellow make orange; yellow and blue make green; and red and blue make purple. These six colors are the colors of the rainbow.

Arranging them in the same order as in a rainbow, but in a circle, produces a useful device known as a "color wheel." Even though you will not have to mix all your colors yourself from the primary hues, a color wheel allows you to see immediately how colors relate to each other. Complementary colors are those that are directly opposite each other on the wheel—orange is the complementary of blue, purple of yellow, green of red, and so on.

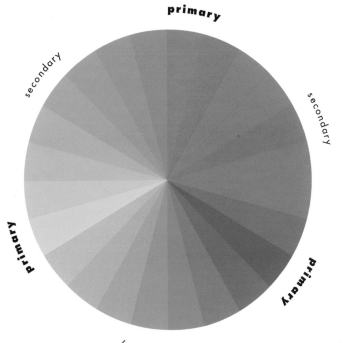

Simple and complex colors

The hues on the color wheel are bright, intense, and uncomplicated, and their tints—to which white has been added—are equally clean and clear. All of these are known as "simple colors." They are ideal for children's rooms but are often used in a variety of other fresh, cheerful interior schemes.

Complex colors are not found on the color wheel. Sophisticated, subtle, and muted, they include such shades as duck egg blue, teal blue, gray-blue, olive green, and garnet red, as well as all the earth reds, oranges, pinks, browns, and yellows. They can be made by adding an earth pigment (e.g., umber, ocher, sienna)—this is sometimes known as

A simple color is a primary color plus white. This pretty sitting room is relaxing because of the gentle pastel colors used on the walls and in the fabrics, which evoke a feeling of innocence and nostalgia.

Country simplicity with a touch of sophistication is created in this hallway. The blue is mixed using primary blue and white, with a small amount of umber. The green has been made in the same way, using primary green rather than blue.

An elegant bathroom created by using natural colors and materials. The burnt orange is an earth color, not a fresh citrus orange. This color scheme, along with the texture of the wall and the green verdigris of the bath, hints at other cultures and times past.

The colors used here are not as complex as the bathroom (left). The choice of colors may look deceptively simple, but the lime yellow, combined with splashes of olive, purple, and pink, gives the room an offbeat sophistication.

"dirtying" or "knocking back" the color. Black can be added to achieve this effect, but it is likely to make the color dull and is therefore not advisable. To quiet a color without muddying it, a little of its complementary can be added. If you are using a complex color and you know what colors it is made from—for example, if a teal blue has been made from viridian green combined with lemon yellow and crimson—then using those colors elsewhere in a room will look harmonious while adding a spark to the scheme.

Experimenting with mixtures of complementaries can lead to some delightful colors. In theory, mixing two complementaries together in equal amounts produces black, but because pigments are involved, the result is usually brown. For really useful neutrals like grays and light browns, which will work harmoniously, combine equal amounts of two complementaries to make the color as dark as possible, then add white. For example, mixing purple with amber yellow and white produces a beautiful taupe gray.

Building in contrasts

When planning a decorating scheme, you need to take into account the amount of contrast, not just of color but also of tone. A color's tone is determined by its intensity—how light or dark it is—and how much white is in it.

Picture a room or a collection of color swatches as a black-and-white photograph and its tones will be instantly revealed.

A simple trick for checking whether the tones in a room are in balance is to half-close your eyes and see if any color jumps out at you. Some tonal contrast is necessary, but if there is too much, the effect can be jarring, particularly in a room that is supposed to be restful.

In a bedroom you could create a calm, tranquil effect by using pale colors that are similar in tone or by using different tones of colors that are adjacent to each other on the color wheel. If the effect is too bland, a small amount of a bright, contrasting color could be used to give it a lift.

In a kitchen or bathroom, a high-contrast scheme would look dynamic and eye-catching, so you could use colors with a lot of variation in tone

A bedroom decorated with invitingly mellow and soothing colors. The tones of the
main colors are perfectly matched, and white and dark purple edging add a little bite.
Half-close your eyes to test the way the color works.

or a range of contrasting colors in similar tones. If you use very strong colors, however, you will need a lot of white to keep them from being overwhelming.

Complementaries provide the maximum color contrast, and when placed side by side, they enhance each other effectively.

Other contrasting schemes include split-complementary schemes, which combine one color with the two colors adjacent to its complementary on the color wheel, and schemes using colors that are neither complementary nor adjacent to each other on the wheel, such as the three primaries. For all of these, it's best to vary the tones and amounts of the colors, so that one color—preferably the cooler one—predominates.

Red and green are complementaries. If the tones are equal, the effect is alarming, as your eye cannot rest on just one of the colors. The colors in this library work because the reds are deep and rich, while the greens are light and airy.

Combining colors

Colors are not used in isolation. They are always used with other colors and it is this reality that many people wrestle with—which color and which shade of that color will work for their individual living spaces. Below are a few basic combinations to get you started and help you find solutions when you have a striking color in your existing furnishings or accessories—perhaps a green carpet or a purple sofa. Getting the balance of quantities is a matter of trial and error. Usually there is a large amount of one color and less of a second, then perhaps a third color is used in small details. Just one cushion or vase in bright red can make a huge difference.

Hallways, staircases, and recesses can often be overlooked, but they are wonderful places to use lively contrasts and adventurous combinations. In this Malibu house, the woodwork is painted in greens and blues, which make a strong contrast with the vibrant orange walls.

Beach House
2 Green Sea Foam
9 Aquamarine Blue

Arts and Crafts
8 Fern Green
4 Greenery Yellowery

Flowery Bower
9 Apple Green
3 Marigold

Bohemian Rhapsody
2 Viridiana
5 Gainsborough Blue

Florentine Renaissance
6 Majolica Green
8 Medici Red

Persian Palace
9 Copper Green
10 Yellow Ocher

Greens plus

Because this secondary color is made by mixing yellow and blue, the range of greens is very wide, from sharp, acidic, lime greens with a lot of yellow in them to dark forest shades and aquamarine greens that can sometimes be confused with blues. Pure green and pure red, its complementary, are roughly the same in tone, and they work well together. However, to be comfortable to the eye, one color has to be lower in tone than the other.

Offbeat
The unconventional combination of lime green with purple is softened by lightening the lime with white and muting the purple to heather.

Earthy
This muted gray-green is the only earth-colored green. It works well with other earth shades like yellow and coppery red ochers.

Calm
Aquamarines can be clinical and devoid of character. Avoid this by using slightly muted versions, then add old golds and pinkish reds.

Fertile
Bright green can be overwhelming. Lighten it with texture, then add deep burnt orange to the palette.

Blues plus

Like greens, the range of blues is enormous—from deep navy to sharp sky blue. There are several blue pigments that make blue. Cobalt and ultramarine are the nearest to primary blue, but cobalt is slightly greenish and ultramarine slightly reddish. Therefore cobalt is used to make aquamarines and ultramarine to make purplish blues. Blue's complementary is orange, but terra cotta and red ochers can also be used.

Manhattan
3 College Blue
1 Lemon Mousse

Beach House
10 Cerulean Sea Blue
5 Cool Bright Yellow

Elizabethan Pageant
1 Cambridge Blue
2 Ivory

Intriguing

The intensity and darkness of the rich green on the wall is broken up by pictures, using plenty of white throughout the room, and a medium blue and a fresher green on the chairs.

Clarity

To make a positive wake-up call, use a strong, clear blue with other primary colors; white or cream will keep it from becoming overpowering.

African Visions
11 Cloudy Blue
9 Cocoa Bean

Bohemian Rhapsody
7 Pierro Blue
3 Brilliant Green

Cool and airy

Pale blue can look young and innocent, but used with mustard yellow and pale moss green, the effect is more complex and suits both adults and children.

Uncomplicated

Pretty baby blue is matched with pale browns, pale woods, and ivories to make it sophisticated and elegant.

Northern Light
8 Danish Blue
1 Dala Pink

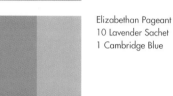

Victorian Parlor
5 Roman Purple
7 Olive Green

Elizabethan Pageant
10 Lavender Sachet
1 Cambridge Blue

Impressionism
8 Purple
2 Citrus Yellow

Mambo Carnival
1 Hummingbird Purple
8 Guatemalan Pink

Out of Africa
3 Madder Pink
1 Maize Yellow

Ballet Russe
2 Scheherezade Purple
9 Elephant Gray

Purples plus

At one end of the range of this secondary color, the purples are bluish, and at the other, they are reddish. The range is smaller than blues and greens, but adding white extends it to include some stunning magenta pinks, lilacs, lavenders, and heathers. The complementary of purple, a dark color, is yellow, which is very light in tone.

Delicate Charm
The delicate warmth of lilac can be enhanced with the addition of gray and white.

Dynamic Statement
Strong, undiluted purple is a dramatic color. To enhance its effect, team it with black, gray, and dusty pinks.

Funky nostalgia
Pale violet can take on an old-fashioned look when partnered with olive greens and creamy colors.

Unconventional
Using muted ocher yellows softens the intensity of clear purples. A little fresh green can also help.

Reds plus

Red is another primary color. Its character changes less across its range than some of the other colors, except when white is added and it changes dramatically to pink. It is indeed a surprise when a bright scarlet red becomes a pretty pastel pink—rather like adding cream to strawberries. Scarlet red and vermilion are at the orange end of red, tomato red is in the middle of the range, while crimson and Bordeaux red are at the bluish end.

Pacific Islands
1 Hibiscus Red
10 Gauguin Blue

Chinatown
1 Emperor Red
6 Imperial Yellow

Neoclassical
8 Aubusson Pink
4 Sandstone

Glam Diva
2 Schiaparelli Pink
1 Truffle Brown

African Visions
4 Ghana Red
3 Clearwater Green

Majestic splendor
Regal magenta pinks and reddish purples look stunning paired with a clear, slightly lemony yellow and gold.

Confidence
Red's strength needs another powerful color to balance it. Black works well and can be used with white and other bright colors.

Balance of power
Strong red is a ubiquitous Asian color—balance it with smaller amounts of black, white, and the primaries yellow and blue.

Feminine power
Give strong, vivid pinks—usually a frivolous color— a serious note by partnering them with chocolate brown, grays, or black.

Rural Retreat
9 Spanish Pink
1 Eucalyptus Green

Pacific Islands
4 Guava Orange
9 Lagoon Blue

Chinatown
7 Mandarin Orange
11 Pale Yellow

Bollywood
6 Orange Flame
1 Festival Pink

Bauhaus
9 Ginger
10 Green Tea

Mambo Carnival
5 Sunset Orange
11 Electric Blue

Bohemian Rhapsody
9 Rust Red
4 Poppy Red

Oranges plus

There are no real orange pigments, only earth pigments—such as burnt sienna—which make earthy brownish oranges, so the range is small. Because orange is a secondary color, it can be made by mixing vermilion red with yellow. The complementary of orange is blue.

Electric Charge

Orange and bright pink are an unlikely combination—many think they clash. As long as the tones are kept similar, the partnership has a zingy snap that will keep you awake.

Rustic and mellow

Terra cotta is a deep earthy orange and has been one of the most popular colors for many years. Use it with mellow copper and blue green, reminiscent of verdigris.

Saucy sensuality

Use fruity orange with lemon yellow and raspberry pink to produce a sensuous combination of colors for a bedroom.

Gentle

The clear, mango orange teamed with lagoon blue makes a clean, fresh combination that is modern and easy to live with.

Yellows plus

Yellow, being a primary color, cannot be mixed from other pigments. The range—which includes lemon yellow, warm buttery yellows, rich mango yellows, greenish mustard yellows, and dark sandy ochers—quickly dissolves into oranges or greens. Yellow's complementary is purple.

Don't look back
Pale lemony yellow is fresh and cool—combine it with spearmint green and pale blue-grays to keep the cool look.

Controlled disorder
Yellow ocher is a mellow but bright color that works especially well with dusty pinks and knocked-back blues.

Carefree
Strong bright yellow, the color of buttercups and egg yolks, can be hard to live with—it needs white, pinks, and a large airy space to make it work.

Intense
Warm yellow veering toward orange calls for other bright colors and creates a happy carnival effect. Bright pinks are particularly effective.

Hippie Chic
1 Mellow Yellow
11 Denim Blue

African Visions
6 Yellow Earth
8 Ghana Red

Mambo Carnival
4 Hot Yellow
9 Carnival Pink

Rock and Roll
1 Sharp Lemon
10 China Green

Impressionism
1 Sunflower Yellow
9 Picasso Pink

Early American
5 Pale Yellow
1 Dusty Green

Stone-ground
4 Leather Brown
3 Straw

African Visions
2 Wet Clay
11 Cloudy Blue

Utilitarian
4 Cocoa
6 Lime-Peel Green

Early American
3 Brick Dust
2 Gray-Green

Chicago Deco
8 Vanilla
10 Lake Gray

Victorian Parlor
9 Chocolate Brown
4 Lavender Sachet

Browns plus

These are some of the most important colors of all, as they make neutral colors, particularly when mixed with white. Wood accounts for a lot of the brown in our interiors, so understanding browns is important. Browns are complex colors and can have a pink, red, yellow, or even a greenish tinge.

Responsive
Soft antelope brown is a welcoming, yet compelling color. Combine it with pale blue to bring out the most of its appeal.

Enhancing
Bring out the warmth of terra-cotta colors, including old brickwork, by contrasting with a natural green.

Clean materials
The brown of beech wood is a pale, creamy orange, making it a perfect partner for the cool gray of stainless steel and aquamarines.

Earthy
Dark, muddy browns and tans made from various ochers make a rich backdrop. Combine with cream and other neutrals to complete the theme.

Grays plus

Grays provide another way of creating neutrals and are very important. They can be made by mixing black and white, or more interestingly, by mixing two complementaries. Grays are immensely versatile and can be used to offset a range of colors, from pale cool aquamarines to deep, earthy reds.

Ballet Russe
9 Elephant Gray
8 Lime Juice

Neoclassical
3 Gentleman's Gray
12 Bordeaux Red

Chicago Deco
11 Silver
6 Egyptian Azure

Stone-ground
1 Slate
2 French Mustard

Northern Light
11 Gray Light
3 + Ocher Yellow

Simply Japanese
4 Enamel Gray
1 Cherry Blossom Pink

Tonal

A clean, cool, pale gray made with blue works well with cool yellow, as they are similar tones. Set it against deep red for warmth and black to balance.

Crisp

Dark gray has the formality of a gentleman's suit. Use with gentle lilacs, pinks, and white to inject some warmth.

Modern

Stainless steel or aluminum is linked to the rest of an interior by using medium and pale grays. Aquamarines add color without undermining the cool, metallic look.

Relaxing

An old gray made with a lot of blue and muddied with warm brown is cozy. Use it with soft blues, yellows, and white for a light room.

Choosing a theme

I have chosen thirty-one themes to cover the main areas of decorating and the full range of colors. Some of the themes are geographical in origin, while others are historical. Artists and artistic movements have inspired a few themes, while nature provided the palettes for others.

If you see a particular theme you like, take that as your starting point. Cross-references are given to other, similar themes, which you may also like.

Conservative

Use these simple blues and yellows with white and gold for classic comfort. Adding touches of gold in the room and using good quality fabrics and finishes are important to make this look work.

Minimalist

A minimalist theme demands only a few colors and patterns, and predominantly plain furniture. Variation is provided by using texture on the various grays. A small addition of deep red brings the whole room to life.

When choosing a theme, you also need to think about how the room is used, which of your existing furnishings you want to include, and how much light the room gets. A dark room that gets little sun needs vibrant colors with strong contrasts.

If the room doesn't get much sunlight, use pale, warm colors with a touch of a vibrant hue. In a room that catches the sun all day, cool colors work well; combine them with plenty of white if the climate is hot.

The four bedrooms below each have a distinctive theme. Colors and themes are, of course, inextricably linked. Using certain colors can lead naturally to a particular theme, as illustrated by the hot pinks in the Indian-style bedroom below left.

Flamboyantly Exotic

The rich colors of Indian sari materials are deeply inviting. Shocking pink, orange, and yellow materials create a flamboyant and colorful room. Use if you want to make a bold statement.

Eastern Elegance

A piece of furniture may spark off ideas for a color theme. This room above, for example, is based around furniture collected from the Middle East. Pale, aquamarine walls pick out items in the room and unite the look.

The schemes

The color schemes in this book are divided into two categories: simple colors are bright, intense, and uncomplicated, and their tints—to which white has been added—are equally clean and clear. Complex colors are sophisticated, subtle, and muted. They include such shades as duck egg blue, gray-blue, olive green, as well as earth reds, oranges, pinks, browns, and yellows.

Every palette has been hand painted, occasionally resulting in slight variations of the same color. Colors also change according to the colors around them. Some of the pure colors have been lightened with white (marked with a +) and their depth will vary according to how much white has been added. Black and white appear throughout the palettes, but for the purposes of this book, they are not treated as colors.

simple colors

complex colors

Beach House

These are not the colors of tropical beaches, but of beaches where the sun is warm but not searing hot—the colors of fishermen's boats, sailing tackle, lighthouses, beach huts, seagulls, and pretty, painted harborside villages, whether on Cape Cod or in Cornwall, England. Fresh, airy, and clean as a summer breeze, they bring to mind rock pools, pebbles, sea, and sand. Use maritime blues, such as navy, and watery aquamarines with sandy ochers, pale but sunny yellows, and bleached, driftwood whites. The general feel is mellow, with little contrast between the colors except for the occasional red or strong blue. Surfaces and fabrics are matte, so use cotton, canvas, textured or crackled paintwork, and simple designs like stripes and polka dots.

The compact design of this room in a Southern California home makes it feel like a galley kitchen. The nautical atmosphere is accentuated by the paint in watery green and aquamarine of the same tones and by the yacht on the dividing wall.

See also
Rural Retreat,
Early American,
Impressionism.

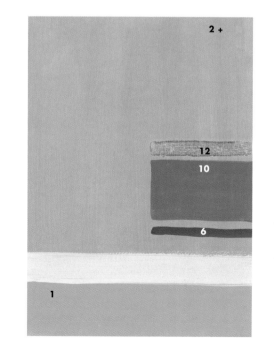

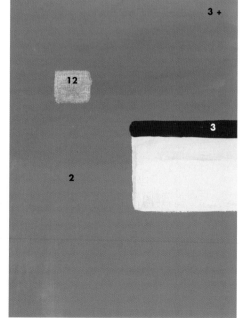

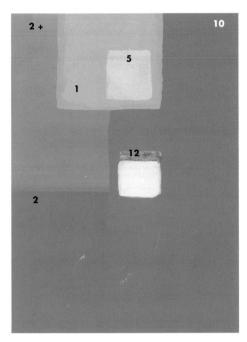

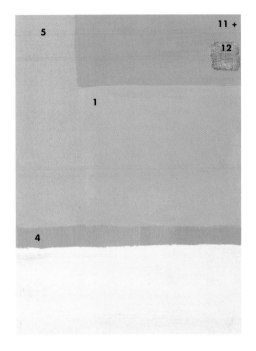

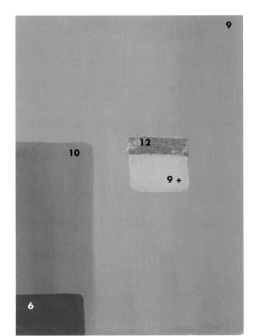

1 Yellow Sunshine

2 Green Sea Foam

3 Sailor Blue

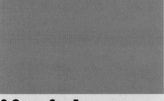

4 Yellow Ocher

5 Cool Bright Yellow

6 Dark Blue Green

Beach House

A deep golden yellow sofa helps to soften the cool airiness of the room, and adds an offbeat look.

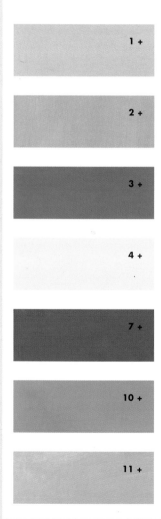

ADDING WHITE

Below you can see what colors 1, 2, 3, 4, 7, 10 and 11 from the palettes look like when white is added to them.

1 +

2 +

3 +

4 +

7 +

10 +

11 +

3 +

7 +

2

6

11 +

11

5

1

1 +

2

8

3 +

4 +

10 +

3 +

7 +

10

4

7 Red Sails

8 Teal Blue

9 Aquamarine Blue

10 Cerulean Sea Blue

11 Sea Moss Green

12 Stainless Steel

Flowery Bower

The fresh spring colors and golden light of an English garden are the inspiration for this delicate, fragrant palette. Unlike the harsh colors of tropical flowers, these light-imbued shades are soft, ranging from apple green and pale primrose yellow to rose pink and lavender: clear, clean, primary and secondary colors to which white has been added. For a more modern interpretation, inject splashes of fiery fuchsia, apricot orange, bright daffodil yellow, delphinium blue, and the vivid green of grass after a rainfall. Green has to play a large part in this theme for obvious reasons. No garden or bouquet of flowers would be complete without deep to bright green foliage to act as a foil for the bevy of bright colors. Keep the colors close in tone to avoid any discordant combinations.

A number of fabrics have been used in the room, including velvet, raffia, silk, and wool, to re-create garden textures like velvety petals and shiny leaves. The vivid, eccentric green on the frame of this traditional sofa contrasts beautifully with the velvet marigold of its seat and cushions.

See also
**Rococo,
Candy Jar,
Bauhaus.**

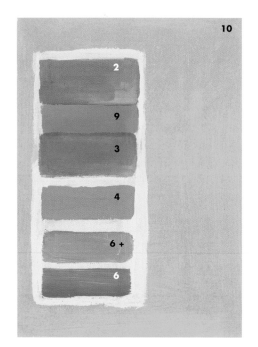

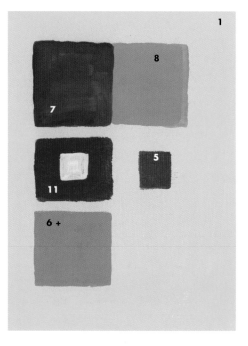

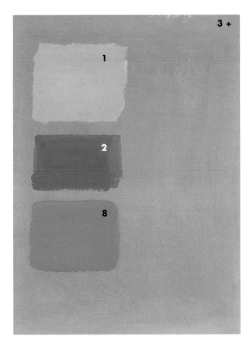

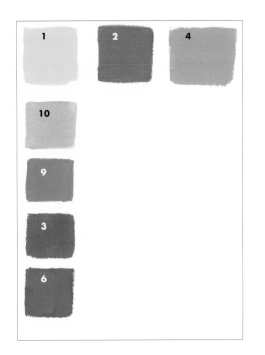

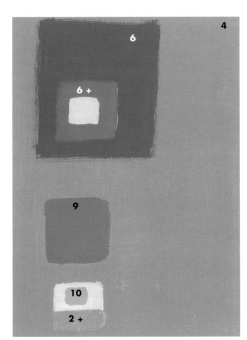

1 Old Rose Pink

2 Mallow Pink

3 Marigold

4 Lilac Blossom

5 Poppy Red

6 Cornflower Blue

Flowery Bower

The garden has been brought indoors with an array of flowery colors. A palette of soft sage green, warm honeysuckle yellow, and old rose pink has been used in connecting rooms to create a tranquil vista. The gently color-washed walls and primrose-yellow woodwork continue the calm, relaxing theme. The whole effect is heightened by adding sparkling touches of color around the room. The softly faded jeweled colors of the Persian carpets serve to link the gentle paint scheme with the bright accents, such as the scarlet plaid throw and the bright orange cushions.

ADDING WHITE

Below you can see what colors 2, 3 and 6 from the palettes look like when white is added to them.

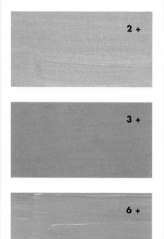

2 +

3 +

6 +

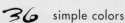

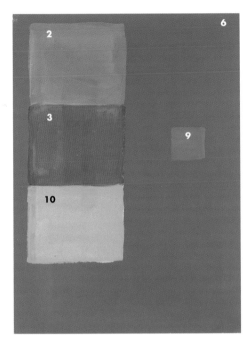

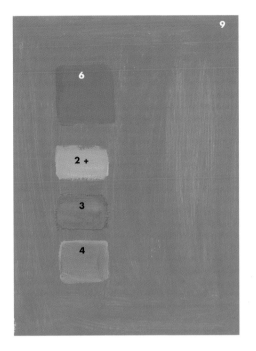

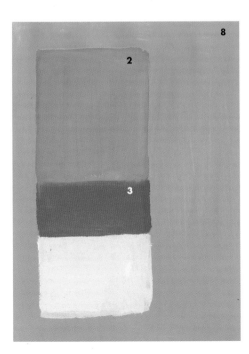

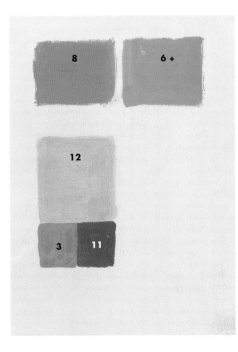

7 Bay Leaf

8 Sage Green

9 Apple Green

10 Daffodil Yellow

11 Autumn Tan

12 Dark Sand

37

Manhattan

This is a classy city look, soothing but not totally relaxed. Think crisp, white shirts, linen, and cashmere. The color scheme has just two main colors plus white. The colors are elegant and clean—one is a darker version of a primary color and the other a paler version, such as navy blue with a warm medium blue that has been softened by the addition of a little white. Generally the colors are slightly cool—lemon yellows, fresh greens, pale blues, strawberry pinks—and the tones are well defined and contrasted. Touches of gold or silver, such as frames and lamps, will add an air of refinement to an otherwise simply colored interior. To keep the look from being too feminine, add weight with grays and eggplants. Matte or semimatte is the finish on paintwork, and fabrics are good-quality cottons and linens.

Ruffled headings and neat edging in a darker-toned blue enhance the distinct contrast between the colors. Touches of gold and crystal offset the hard-edged feel of the room and give it a sophisticated look.

See also
Candy Jar,
Rococo,
Bauhaus.

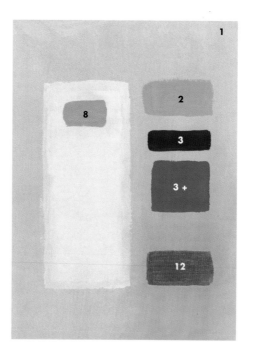

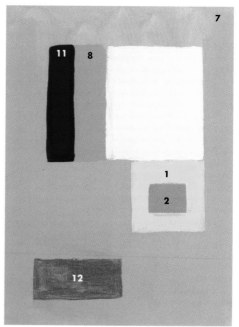

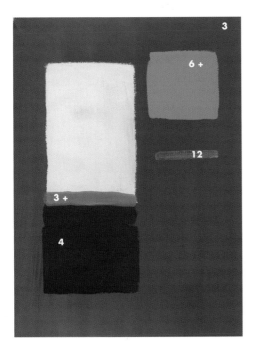

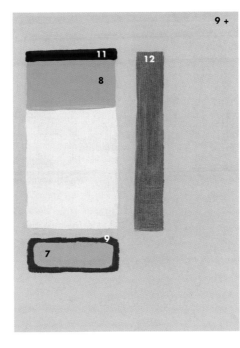

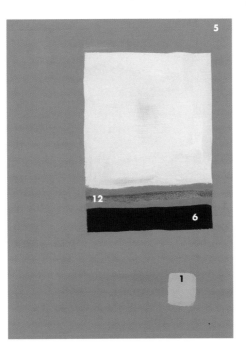

1 Lemon Mousse

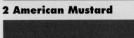

2 American Mustard

3 College Blue

4 Navy Blue

5 Clean Green

6 Bottle Green

Manhattan

The balance of color is almost equal between the blue, yellow, and white in this cottage bedroom. The only pattern is the simple pinstripe on the fabric.

ADDING WHITE

Below you can see what colors 1, 2, 3, 4, 5, 6 and 9 from the palettes look like when white is added to them.

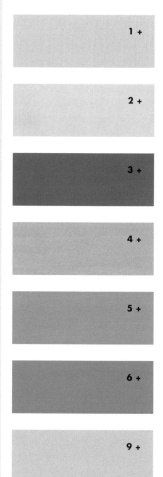

1 +

2 +

3 +

4 +

5 +

6 +

9 +

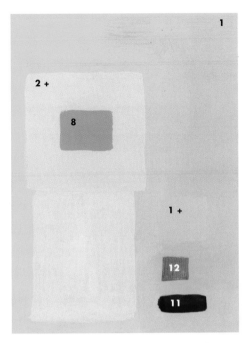

1

2 +

8

1 +

12

11

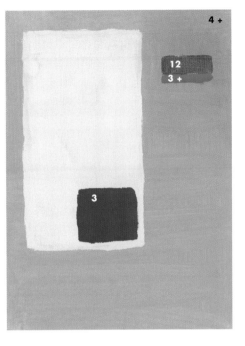

4 +

12
3 +

3

5 +

5

12

10

6 +

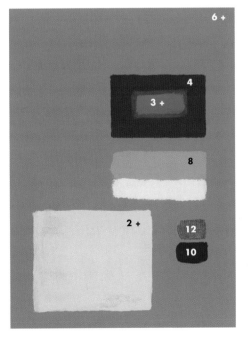

6 +

4

3 +

8

2 +

12

10

7 Cement Gray

8 Putty Gray

9 Strawberry

10 Redwood

11 Eggplant

12 Gold

41

Candy Jar

These bright colors work wonderfully in the kitchen, brightening everyone's morning.

Use vivid, eye-catching colors inspired by packaging, plastic toys, sports gear, and candy. These are the colors of the supermarket, where shelves are stacked with many colors, all shouting for attention. They have an inviting appeal and make no apologies for their brightness. The overall effect is clean, uncluttered, ordered, and uplifting. The Candy Jar palette consists of primary and secondary colors with some strong pastels. They can border on gaudy, kitschy, or childlike, so they need to be handled carefully. Use these colors with plenty of black and white to make clear, uncluttered, quiet areas. Surfaces should be glossy rather than matte—materials like chrome and glass work well here. Add accessories in strong, bold, modern colors.

See also
Flowery Bower,
Rococo,
Rock and Roll.

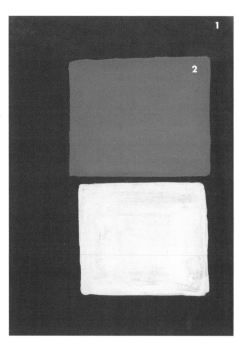

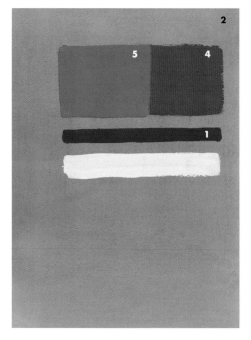

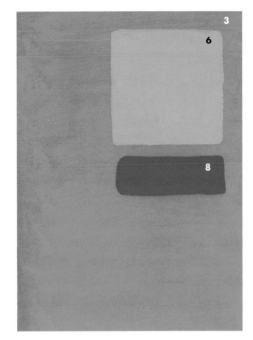

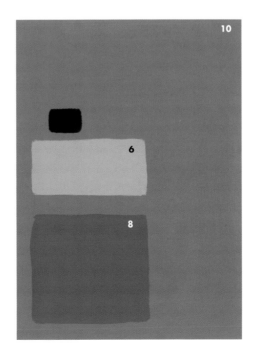

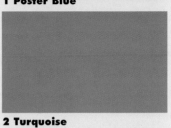

1 Poster Blue

2 Turquoise

3 Orange Tangerine

4 Poster Red

5 Fluorescent Pink

6 Lemon Yellow

Candy Jar

This is a cheerful and uplifting kitchen because of the use of many primary and secondary colors, and the strong contrasts created by setting them against white to give an airy feel. The harlequin-colored tiling goes well with the black-and-white flooring, the jelly-colored resin knobs, and the chandelier.

ADDING WHITE

Below you can see what color 3 from the palettes looks like when white is added to it.

3 +

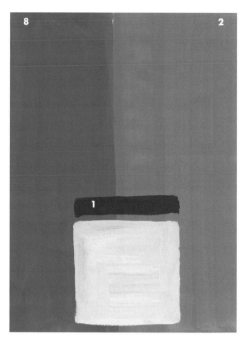

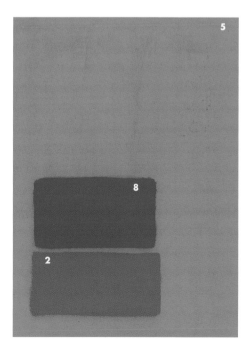

7 Egg Yolk

8 Emerald Green

9 Intense Pink

10 Light Green

11 Deep Aqua

ROCOCO

The style of country houses and palaces all over Europe in the first half of the eighteenth century was graceful, elegant, and playful. The colors matching this mood are frothy pastels in coral pinks, gray-blues, soft greens, lavenders, and pale yellows. As they are pale, several can be used together—but it is generally best to pick out one color and a counter color, usually the complementary, to enliven the scheme and give the room focus. Avoid any hard contrasts, as the aim is to keep the look sophisticated and restful. Use paint with a soft sheen on the walls or line them with silk or a light glazed cotton. To add the finishing touches, use gold and silver in abundance on furniture, ornately carved frames, and decorative china. Fabrics should be light and soft, with delicate patterns. Curving shapes are the order of the day.

Pinks, both pale and strong, are used with their complementary, soft green, and duck egg blue in this pretty, rococo-inspired living room. The many patterns pick up on the main colors, while allowing others to be introduced. The result is both colorful and restful.

See also
Candy Jar,
Manhattan,
Flowery Bower,
Neoclassical.

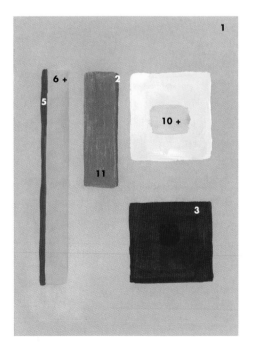

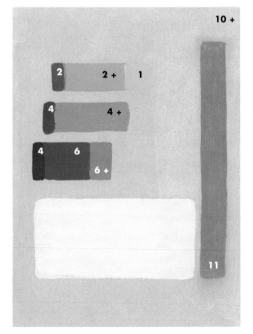

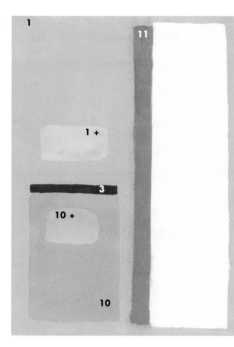

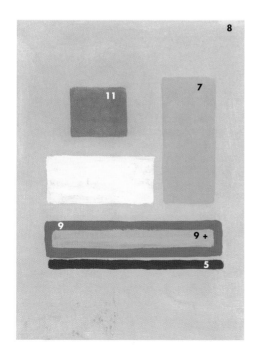

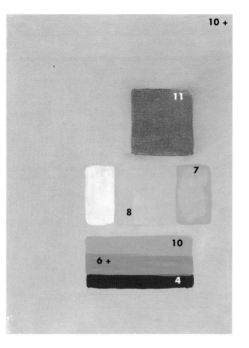

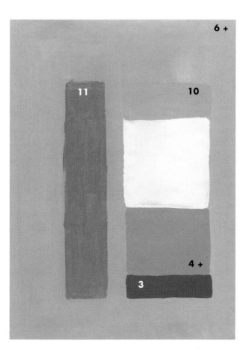

1 Shell Pink

2 Terra-Cotta Pink

3 Bordeaux Red

4 Darkest Violet

5 Prussian Blue

6 Powder Blue

Rococo

A modern variation of rococo, evident in the flowing scroll design of the table legs. Yellow has been heightened, used with its complementary, lilac, and softened by white.

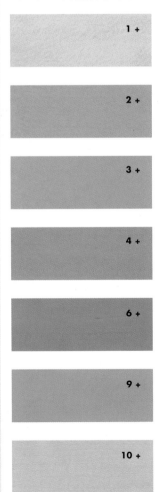

ADDING WHITE

Below you can see what colors 1, 2, 3, 4, 6, 9 and 10 from the palettes look like when white is added to them.

1 +

2 +

3 +

4 +

6 +

9 +

10 +

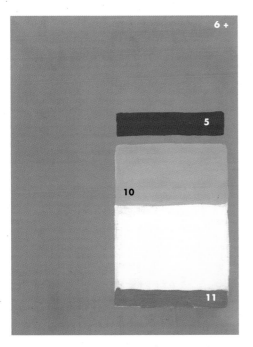

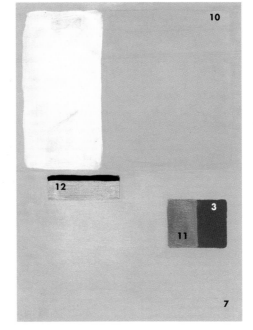

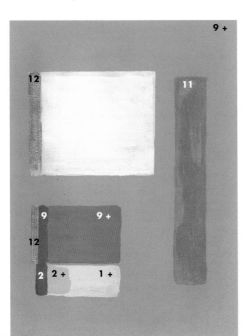

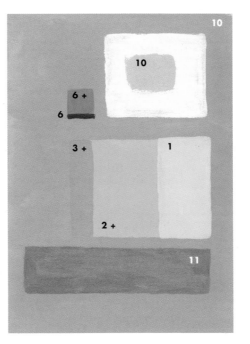

7 Primrose Yellow

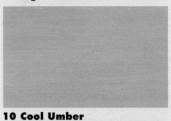

8 Pale Golden Yellow

9 Sage Green

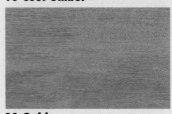

10 Cool Umber

11 Gold

12 Silver

49

Rock and Roll

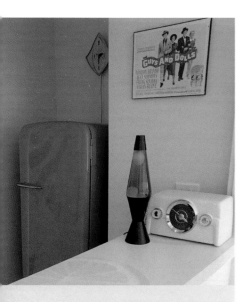

These are the colors of the 1950s, the dawn of a new era that emerged from the war with a new exuberance and irreverence. The colors are bright, uncompromising, unsophisticated primaries and secondaries—sometimes sharp and shockingly fluorescent, sometimes sweet and pastel, but always uncomplicated. This is a palette that is deliberately simple and loud, full of bright colors "straight from the bottle," a release from the restricted palette of the war years. Shocking pinks, pale sweet pinks, sky blues, lemon yellows, lime greens, and lipstick reds are the trademark colors of the time. These are counterbalanced with white, black, and gray to create a clean, upbeat, and optimistic look. Black is favored as a trim for almost any color.

A cool kitchen with items from the 1950s and 1960s uses spearmint green and brilliant yellow. Simple materials, including glass and vinyl, and plastic finishes complete the theme.

See also
Candy Jar,
Glam Diva,
Rococo.

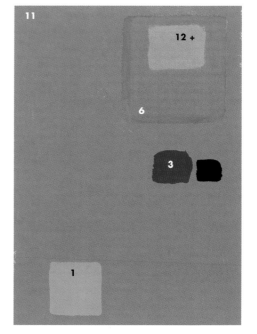

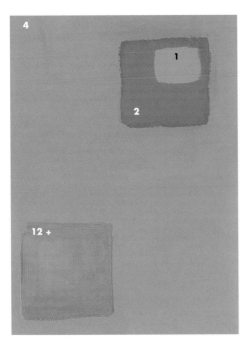

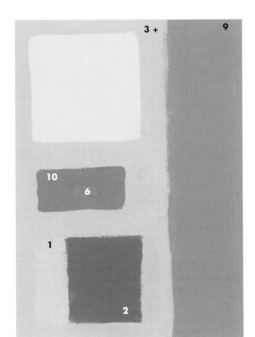

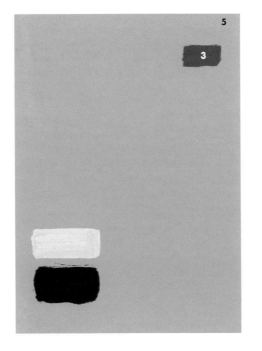

1 Sharp Lemon

2 Orange Zing

3 Sputnik Red

4 Neon Blue

5 Baby Blue

6 Shocking Pink

Rock and Roll

Orange and bright pink are an
unlikely combination. However, as
long as the tones are kept similar, the
combination has a zingy snap that's
guaranteed to keep you awake.

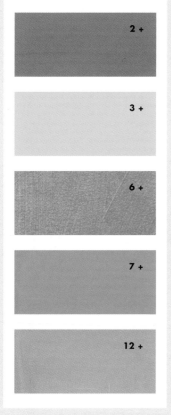

ADDING WHITE

Below you can see what colors 2, 3, 6,
7 and 12 from the palettes look like
when white is added to them.

2 +

3 +

6 +

7 +

12 +

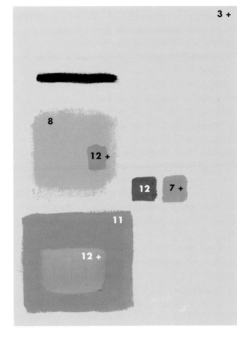

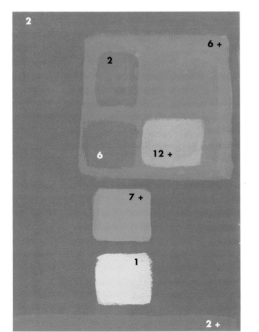

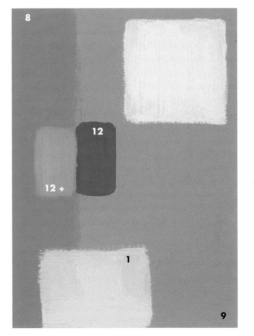

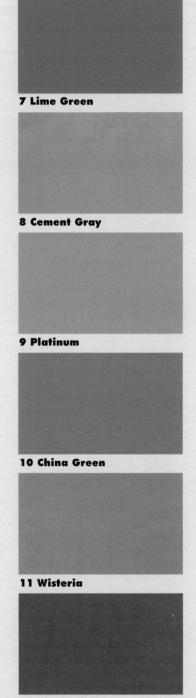

7 Lime Green

8 Cement Gray

9 Platinum

10 China Green

11 Wisteria

12 Cherry Red

Impressionism

For Monet, Renoir, and the other impressionist artists, color was king. These late nineteenth-century painters were innovators, painting directly from nature, capturing the changing effects of light, and juxtaposing fragments of paint on the canvas. Many of them worked in France, where they were inspired by the clear light, the colorful Provençal fabrics, and the painted furniture. Monet used a similar style in his dining room at Giverny, and in Normandy, he painted the walls and furniture in pale chrome yellow with the moldings picked out in medium chrome yellow. Cobalt blue and white fireplace tiles and china provided a crisp contrast. For your own impressionist theme, make a backdrop for other colors using slightly mellowed primaries—though not complex colors, they are sophisticated.

To achieve radiant yellow and reds using earth colors, the quality has to be good, especially when a little white is to be added. This style has its roots in peasant culture, so use solid, rustic furniture with rough finishes and ceramics with matte or slightly glazed surfaces.

See also
Bauhaus,
Pacific Islands.

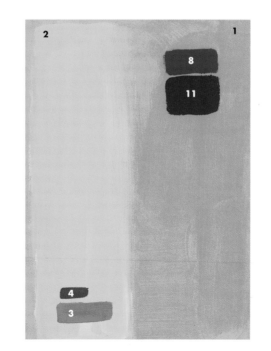

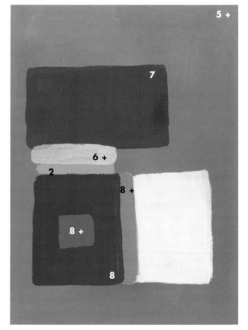

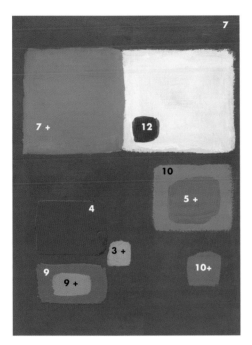

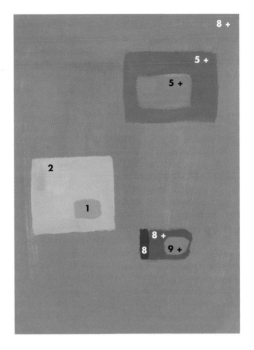

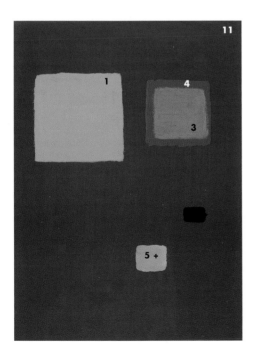

1 Sunflower Yellow

2 Citrus Yellow

3 Tangerine

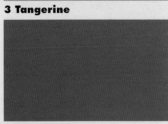

4 Terra Cotta

5 Paris Blue

6 Ocher Yellow

55

Impressionism

This cottage uses the glorious colors of an impressionist painting. The warm yellow walls and rosy earth pink in the far room provide a brilliant backdrop to rich reds and greens.

ADDING WHITE

Below you can see what colors 3, 5, 6, 7, 8, 9 and 10 from the palettes look like when white is added to them.

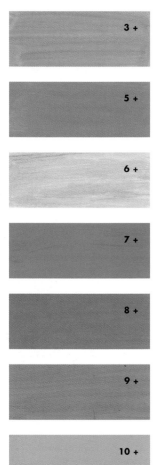

3 +

5 +

6 +

7 +

8 +

9 +

10 +

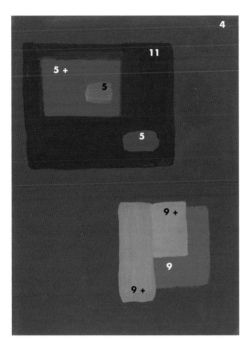

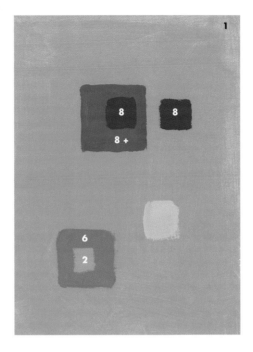

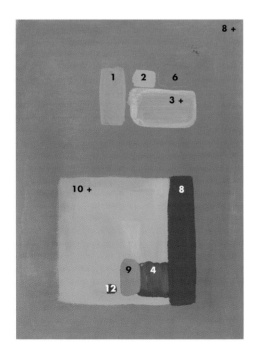

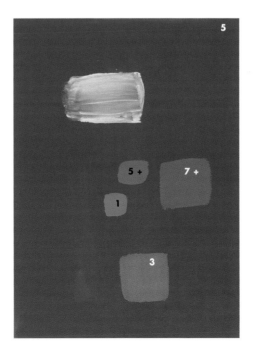

7 Emerald Green

8 Purple

9 Picasso Pink

10 Summer Green

11 Matisse Blue

12 Claret Red

57

Simply Japanese

A bedroom in an old house in France was given a completely modern renovation inspired by the minimalist look of contemporary Japan.

See also
**Chicago Deco,
Chinatown,
Ballet Russe.**

Marry the colors of old Japan with some from modern Japan to make the traditional minimalist style softer. A ubiquitous color in Japan, strong red has been used with black for everything from old buildings to kimonos and paper lanterns. It is also found with a gingery red on lacquerwork furniture, screens, and tableware. In cool contrast, the soft gray-greens of celadon or jade-green ceramics provide a pleasing balance. With black and white, these make up the backbone of traditional Japanese colors. In modern Tokyo, the colors are enhancements of the traditional ones: red and pale cherry blossom pink becomes bright pink, celadon becomes brilliant emerald green, and ginger becomes orange.

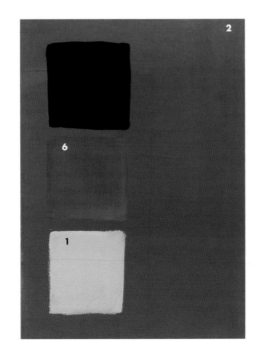

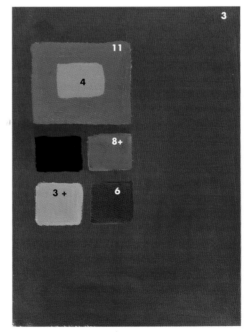

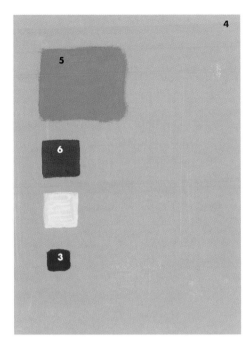

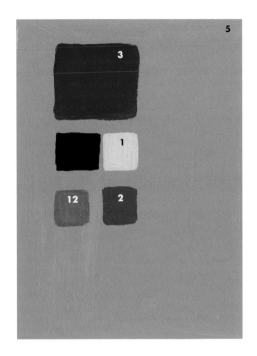

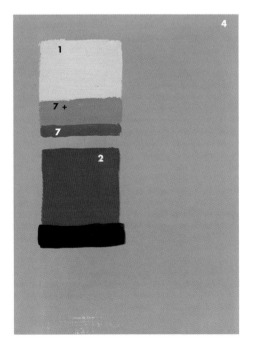

1 Cherry Blossom Pink

2 Spice Red

3 Lacquer Red

4 Enamel Gray

5 Celadon Green

6 Deep Violet

Simply Japanese

The ascetic character of this tall room was accentuated by lowering the focal point—achieved with a deep-colored wood paneling around the bed. Few colors are used, instead the emphasis is on texture and materials. There are strong contrasts, but the delicate, soft fabrics make this a comfortable room. Introduce reds or more contemporary urban colors like pink or orange to make a room like this less stark.

ADDING WHITE

Below you can see what colors 2, 5, 6, 7 and 8 from the palettes look like when white is added to them.

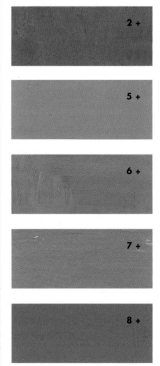

2 +

5 +

6 +

7 +

8 +

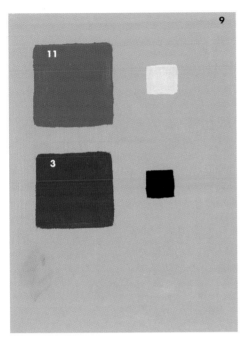

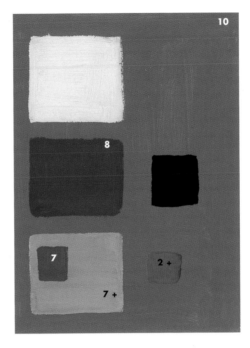

7 Peony Pink

8 Cloisonné Green

9 Pebble Gray

10 Turquoise

11 Charcoal

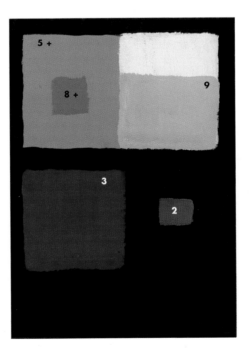

12 Gold

Bauhaus

The Bauhaus was a highly influential German school of architecture and design in the 1920s that pioneered studies of the effects of different combinations of pure color, influencing modern architecture, furniture, and interior design in the United States and Europe. To re-create this clean, architectural look, use pure primaries in large slabs of color, such as on a wall in an otherwise white-painted room or on a piece of furniture. Secondary colors and pale colors are not so apparent, and the only pattern is abstract or geometric. Materials include brick and cement, chrome, leather, and high-quality plastics. One of the school's precepts was that "less is more," so don't fill the room with clutter. When few colors are used, it is important to include textures, such as both smooth and roughcast walls, and both shiny and matte surfaces.

Clear, strong shape is as much a part of the Bauhaus message as color is. With white or cream walls, colors should be bold to make an impact.

See also
Ballet Russe,
Chicago Deco,
Impressionism,
Simply Japanese.

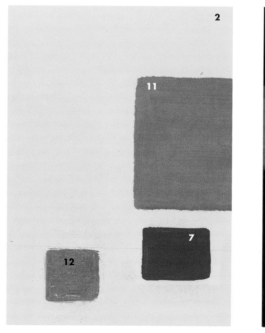

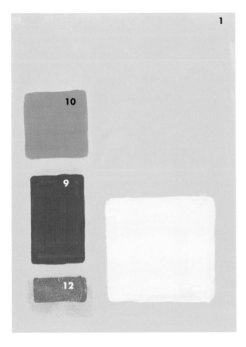

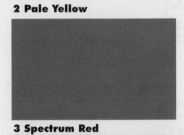

1 Clear Yellow

2 Pale Yellow

3 Spectrum Red

4 Plum Red

5 Sand

6 Steel Gray

Bauhaus

This room has a geometric simplicity, using white walls as a background for abstract slabs of color, like the red sofa with pillows in different solid colors. The only area of pattern is the rug, balanced by the modern print over the fireplace. With so few colors and such strong contrasts, it is essential to use a lot of texture, from the smooth and shiny table to the rough surface of the fireplace.

ADDING WHITE

Below you can see what colors 1 and 2 from the palettes look like when white is added to them.

1 +

2 +

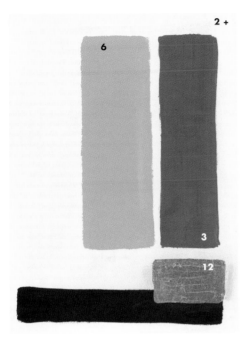

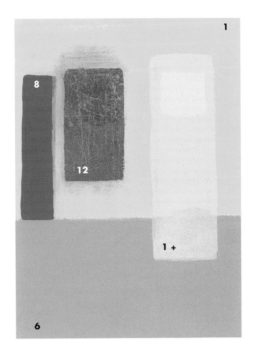

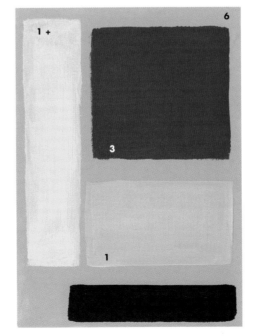

7 Klee Blue

8 Nut Brown

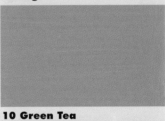

9 Ginger

10 Green Tea

11 Burnt Orange

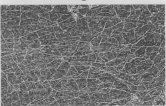

12 Aluminum

65

Pacific Islands

Bright and clear color with lots of white is the signature of this theme inspired by the colors found in a Pacific island paradise: the turquoise of lagoons, the blue of a cloudless sky, hibiscus red, frangipani pink, pineapple yellow, and banana-leaf green. Few colors are used and there is always an abundance of white, so a room decorated in this scheme has a light, airy, spacious feel. Although the colors look as though they have come straight from a child's paint box, they are not overly bold and have a gentle, refreshing quality. This is because the textures are always matte: soft cottons, oiled rather than varnished wood, and natural materials like bamboo and stone.

Unvarnished wood furniture, combined with small ornaments and accessories in yellow, lime, red, and purple, will complement this tropical color scheme perfectly.

See also
**Impressionism,
Bauhaus.**

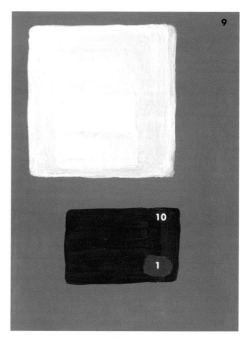

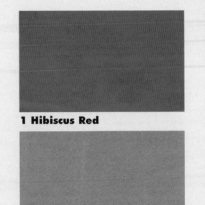

1 Hibiscus Red

2 Frangipani Pink

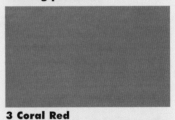

3 Coral Red

4 Guava Orange

5 Mango Yellow

6 Sunshine Yellow

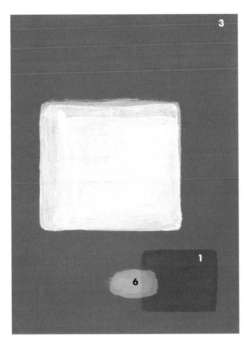

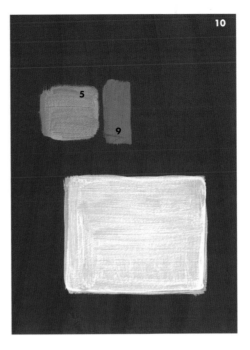

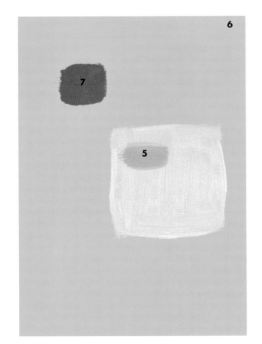

67

Pacific Islands

Clear, citrus accents give a fresh, clean appeal to any room. Here the deep tangerine of the kitchen wall looks wonderfully vibrant when teemed with cool turquoise and warm dusty-pink storage cupboards, and offset by plain white tiles. Natural wood furniture and an array of small ornaments in yellow, lime, red, and purple complement the scheme perfectly and lend it all the richness of a tropical rainbow.

ADDING WHITE

Below you can see what color 5 from the palettes look like when white is added to it.

5 +

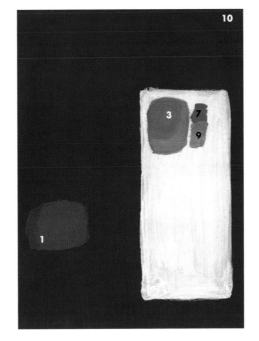

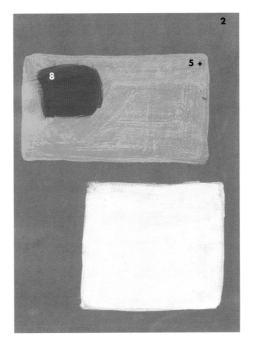

7 Banana Leaf Green

8 Island Green

9 Lagoon Blue

10 Gauguin Blue

69

Chinatown

A visit to Chinatown reveals the glorious hues of traditional and modern Chinese silks and satins, and of old porcelain ginger jars, bowls, and plates. The colors are intense primary hues like Tang yellow (a lemon yellow named after a ceramic glaze developed in China during the Tang dynasty), fiery dragon red, rich midnight blue, and peony pink. Several of these colors can be used together to stunning effect. Pearly grays and silvery whites, rather than harsh whites, are used. To keep the colors from becoming overpowering, use black lacquer furniture. The paintwork and furniture always have a shine, but it is the sheen of traditional lacquerwork rather than a high gloss. For the same reason, fabrics with a sheen, such as silk, satin, and brocade, work well.

This part of the inner room seen on page 72 has the ceiling and walls painted in Chinese red, brightening an otherwise dark room and making it rich and inviting. Painting a dark room white does not add light—the room will merely look gray.

See also
**Simply Japanese,
Ballet Russe.**

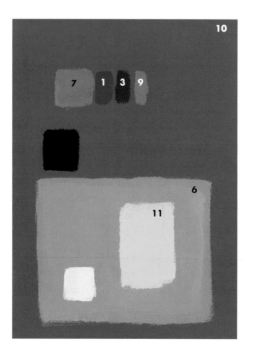

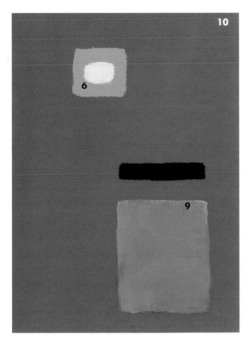

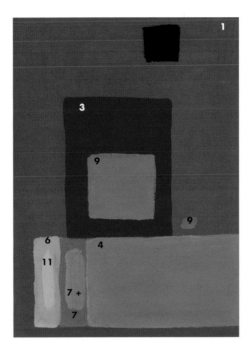

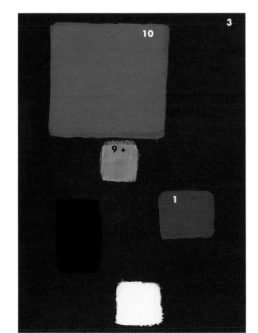

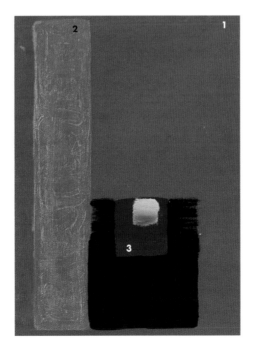

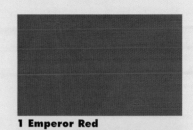

1 Emperor Red

2 Gold

3 Ming Blue

4 Cherry Blossom Pink

5 Bright China Blue

6 Imperial Yellow

Chinatown

This modern interior in Hong Kong is decorated with bright, clear colors inspired by Chinese silks and porcelain. Light and life is given to the room by ceiling lights, the white lampshade, and the floor. In contrast, the light outer room is painted golden yang yellow and decorated with white and vibrant blue. These colors are the primary colors but the room has a sophisticated look. Decorative items are used sparingly to maintain this ambience.

ADDING WHITE

Below you can see what colors 7 and 9 from the palettes look like when white is added to them.

7 +

9 +

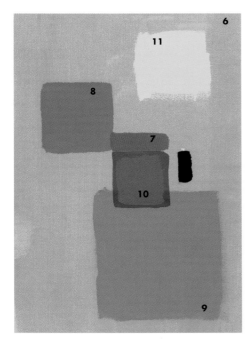

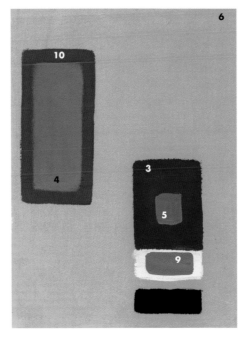

7 Mandarin Orange

8 Dragon Green

9 Turquoise Blue

10 Snapdragon Pink

11 Pale Yellow

Neoclassical

This fin-de-siecle theme reflects the style of the classical world of ancient Greece and Rome, particularly Pompeii. The style is grand and was intended for large rooms, but it can be successfully translated into smaller rooms, though high ceilings are needed for it to work effectively. The colors are often solid, almost primary reds, blues, yellows, purples, and greens, used with off-white and black, and with gold and silver decoration. Use a few colors in a room, with one dominating on the walls. Fabrics to complete this look are generally shiny and luxurious, including damasks, glazed taffetas, and velvets.

In this modern interpretation of a neoclassical style, the stark contrast of the near-black walls and white frames, combined with the almost abstract shapes of the urns, makes a powerful statement. The severity is broken by the introduction of cream and gold, as well as purple silk and a little red in the gilded chairs.

See also
Florentine Renaissance,
Rococo,
Ballet Russe.

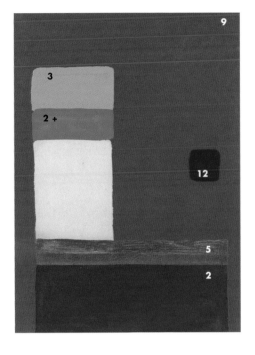

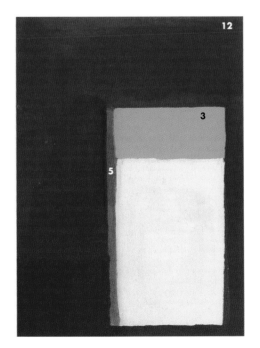

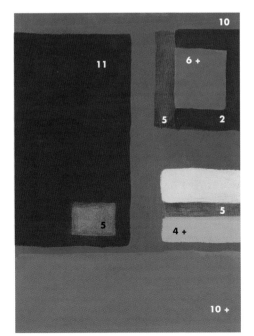

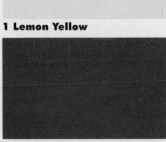

1 Lemon Yellow

2 Empire Blue

3 Gentleman's Gray

4 Sandstone

5 Gold

6 Lavender Blue

75

Neoclassical

Bright yellow walls and a typical neoclassical magenta silk on the chair are cleverly combined with a 1930s art-deco lamp in black and gold and the neoclassical, trophy-style wall

ADDING WHITE

Below you can see what colors 2, 4, 6, 8, 10 and 11 from the palettes look like when white is added to them.

2 +

4 +

6 +

8 +

10 +

11 +

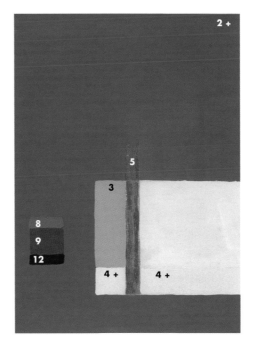

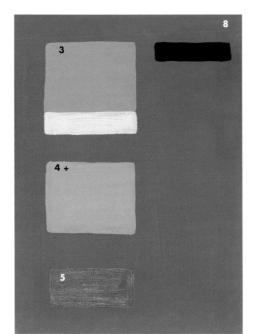

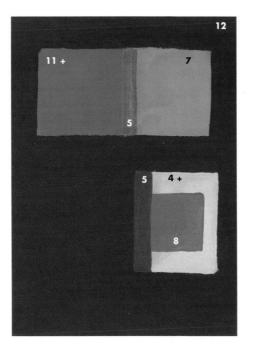

7 Porcelain

8 Aubusson Pink

9 Soldier Red

10 Amethyst

11 Forest Green

12 Bordeaux Red

Bollywood

India is extraordinarily rich in dazzling color but nowhere more so than in the famous movie industry, Bollywood. Its heroes and heroines are clothed in glittering, shimmering costumes, the colors of which have been heightened for maximum effect. These are dynamic, offbeat primaries and secondaries that shout for attention—jewel colors like ruby, emerald, sapphire, amethyst, and topaz, festooned with gold and silver. As an interior scheme, these dazzling colors will have a real impact. Several are used together, but they are often grouped in families, all of a similar tone—blues with turquoise and green, for example, or purples and pinks. Create a strong contrast with white to provide a cool, quiet area. Textures should be shiny, so use sari fabrics with gold and silver.

In this bedroom, the heady mixture of hot colors is based on a delicious saffron yellow painted on the walls and ceiling. This is almost matched in tone by the topaz, amber, burnt orange, and ginger accents. The room has a potent vibrancy due partly to strongly saturated color and partly to the use of two equally toned complementaries, purple and yellow.

See also
Glam Diva,
Mambo Carnival.

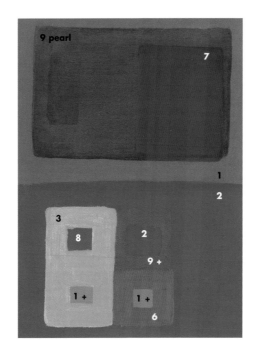

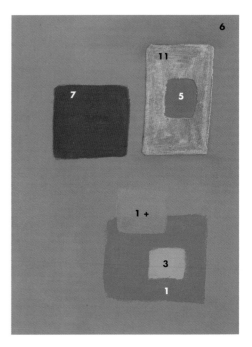

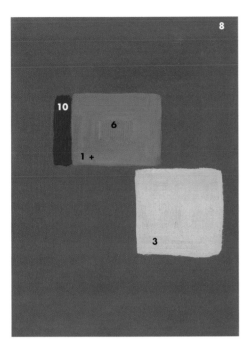

8

10

6

1 +

3

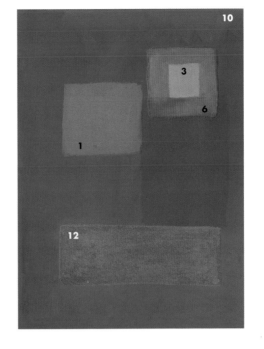

10

3

6

1

12

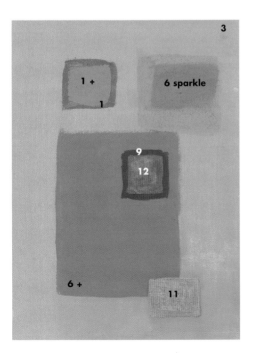

3

1 +

6 sparkle

1

9

12

6 +

11

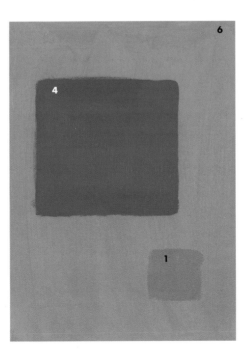

6

4

1

1 Festival Pink

2 Deep Cerise

3 Saffron Lemon

4 Opal Green

5 Leaf Green

6 Orange Flame

Bollywood

The strongly contrasting white, cream, and beige in the luxurious bed offer a cool space in an otherwise very hot room.

TEXTURE

Add an extra dimension of light reflective texture to bright colors with sparkle and shiny two-tone effects to maximize their impact.

5 SPARKLE

6 SPARKLE

9 PEARL

ADDING WHITE

Below you can see what colors 1, 6 and 9 from the palettes look like when white is added to them.

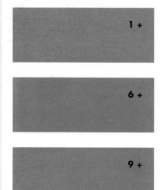

1 +

6 +

9 +

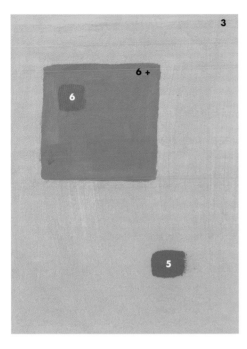

3

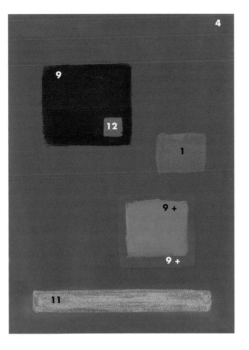

4

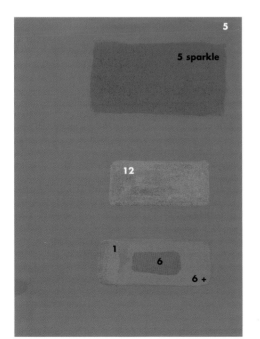

5

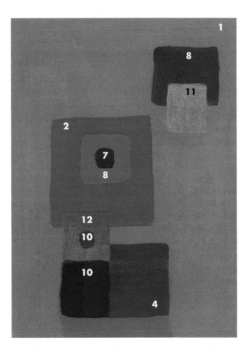

1

7 Temple Red

8 Emerald Green

9 Hill Purple

10 Rajasthan Blue

11 Silver

12 Gold

Glam Diva

This is the ultimate in traditional, uncompromising femininity expressed by every glamorous diva from Marilyn Monroe to Madonna. The combination of colors is striking and the tonal contrasts are strong, so the effect is dramatic and theatrical. Every pink is utilized, especially the hard, brilliant pinks. Made from a crimson base, these are cold colors that slide effortlessly into purple, mauve, lavender, and lilac. In addition, lipstick red is used with powder-puff white, cool aqua blues, crisp lemon yellows, and spearmint greens—all hard and cold. They are matched by a lot of metallics, pearl, and crystal, which give not only a luxurious look, but when used against slabs of bright color, add a lighter touch. With these colors, use rich chocolatey brown, grays, ivory, and creamy white.

Black, white, and ivory objects stand out against the brilliant pink of the walls. A nod to classical design adds an elegant feel to the room.

See also
**Bollywood,
Rock and Roll,
Neoclassical,
Ballet Russe.**

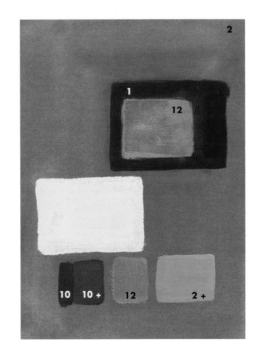

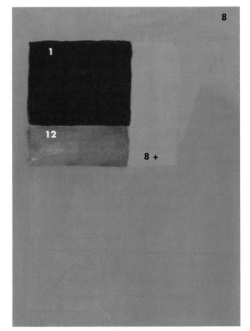

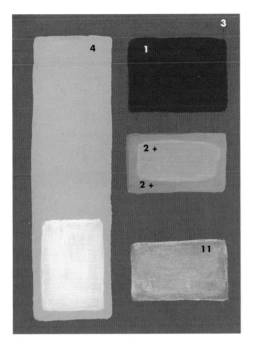

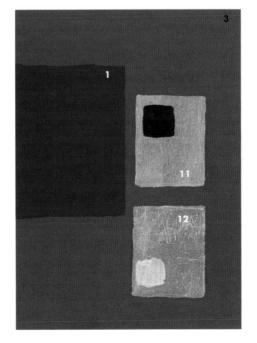

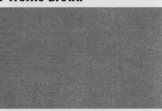

1 Truffle Brown

2 Schiaparelli Pink

3 Lipstick Red

4 Dove Gray

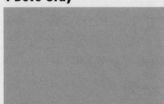

5 Pansy Violet

6 Black Currant

Glam Diva

Here is a room in which to strike a pose and be noticed. The strong cherry pink on the walls and blinds creates a powerful effect in an otherwise neutral-colored room. Curvy furniture, a glass table, and a dripping chandelier counter the hardness. The pale colors further soften the look. The earthy golden yellow on the armchair helps to give the room a certain sophistication.

ADDING WHITE

Below you can see what colors 2, 6, 8, 9 and 10 from the palettes look like when white is added to them.

 2 +

 6 +

 8 +

 9 +

 10 +

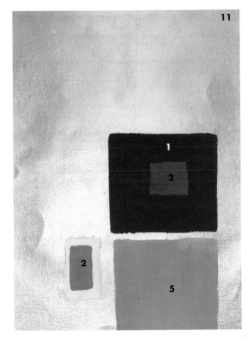

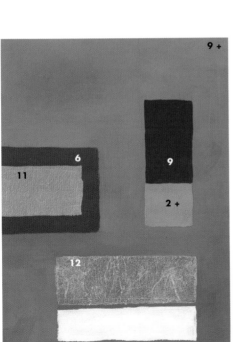

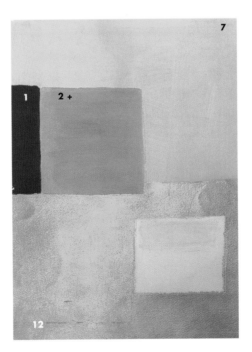

7 Buttercup Yellow

8 Strong Aquamarine

9 Sapphire Blue

10 Mahogany Red

11 Silver

12 Gold

85

Mambo Carnival

The key to the carnival theme is lots of color. Use shocking combinations that almost clash.

See also
Bollywood,
Pacific Islands
Glam Diva.

Tropical fruits and flowers, parrots, Latin-American jazz, and Spanish fiestas have inspired these flamboyant combinations of colors. This is also the palette of Mardi Gras, the carnival famous for its outrageous costumes in exotic colors and materials. Extremely bold primaries, particularly fiery parrot red and pineapple yellow, are used with vibrant secondaries like emerald green, orange, lime green, lemon, bougainvillea purple, and pink. Many colors are often combined to create a strong contrast, for example, hummingbird blue with brilliant pink, or lime green with black and pink. To use this theme in a kitchen, focus on the tropical fruit colors. In a bedroom or dining area, more glamorous effects, like glittery sequins, gold and silver fabrics, and ostentatious feathers, can be used.

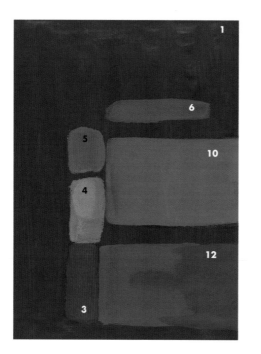

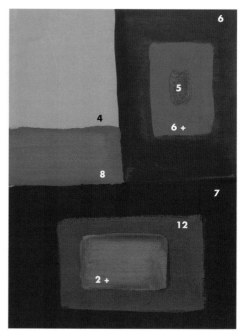

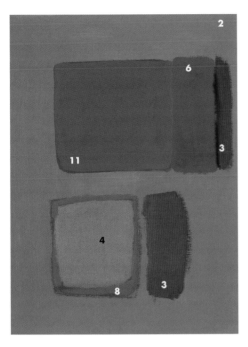

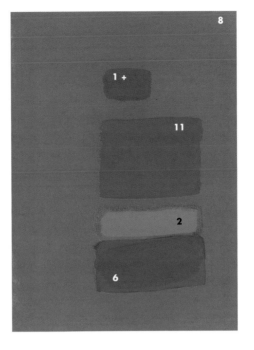

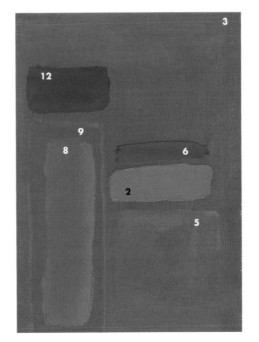

1 Hummingbird Purple

2 Parrot Green

3 Scarlet Red

4 Hot Yellow

5 Sunset Orange

6 Viridian Green

Mambo carnival

The look of this kitchen is essentially based on simple colors, although it also contains slightly more subtle elements. The green of the dresser is mellow, but combined with the orange and pink, the overall color scheme remains a simple one.

ADDING WHITE

Below you can see what colors 2, 6, 11 and 12 from the palettes look like when white is added to them.

2 +

6 +

11 +

12 +

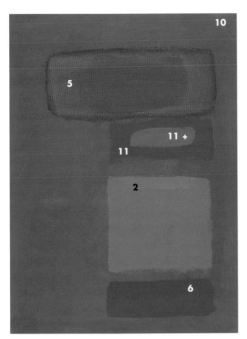

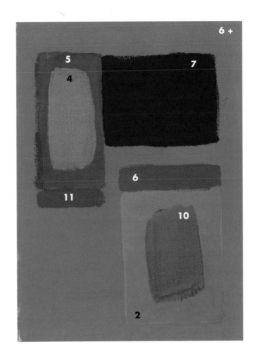

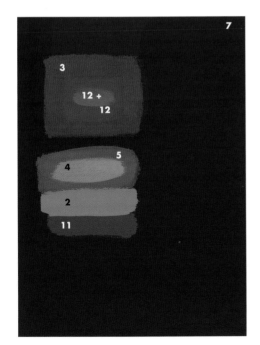

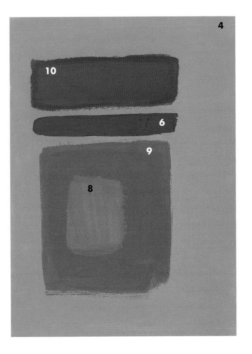

7 Mexican Blue

8 Guatemalan Pink

9 Carnival Pink

10 Jungle Green

11 Electric Blue

12 Dusky Mauve

Stone-ground

This is a detail of the hallway on page 92. A number of different design elements have been brought together here, including Shaker, Native American, Victorian, and African.

See also
African Visions,
Rural Retreat.

Inspired by the natural landscape of clays, stones, and pale woods, these subtle, understated colors include restrained light browns, washed-out blues and greens, and soft grays. Because the colors are all complex and often quite cool and pale, the overall effect is very calming and peaceful. Use off-white and pale blue-grays for a little contrast to prevent a drab effect. The similarities in color and tone mean that texture is particularly important here. Use a flat or semimatte textured paint on the walls, and wax rather than varnish on furniture to give a mellow sheen. Although the colors are sophisticated, they can be used with very unsophisticated finishes. There is a handmade look about the materials—simple cottons, bare wood, and hand-thrown pottery.

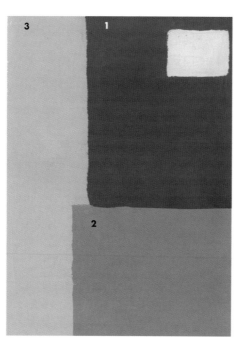

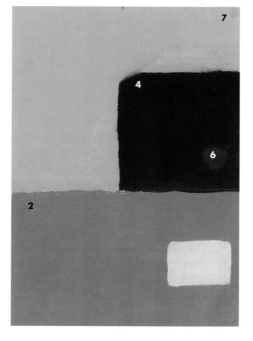

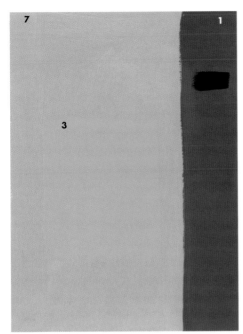

7

3

1

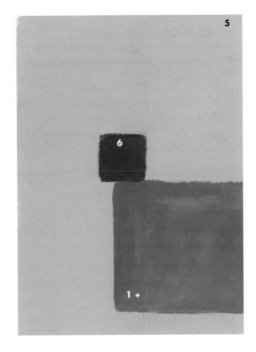

5

6

1 +

3

8

7

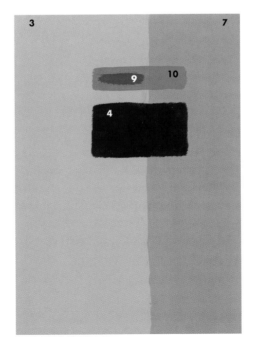

3

7

9   10

4

1 Slate

2 French Mustard

3 Straw

4 Leather Brown

5 Plaster Pink

6 Brick Red

Stone-ground

The dark but vibrant colors of the Victorian floor and stained glass work well, not only with the earthy, nutty colors of the hallway, but also the decorative ethnic elements. Textures are soft, mellow, and natural with a medium sheen rather than a high gloss.

ADDING WHITE

Below you can see what color 1 from the palettes looks like when white is added to it.

1 +

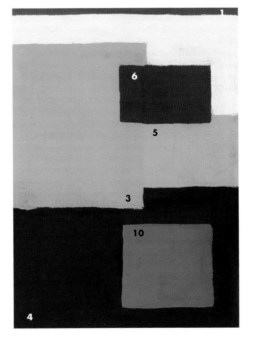

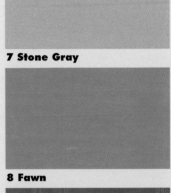

7 Stone Gray

8 Fawn

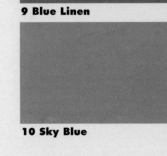

9 Blue Linen

10 Sky Blue

African Visions

African designs have long been an inspiration for decoration and design, particularly after modern artists like Picasso "discovered" them. Many of the colors seen in traditional African pottery and carving come from nature. There are a few bright colors like warm indigo blue and bright red, but generally the palettes used in African interiors are based on complex earth colors. Radiant yellows, ocher reds, oranges, pinkish mauves, chocolate brown, charcoal black, and chalky white are the mainstays of the theme. Few colors are needed for an African-inspired interior, but the textures must be right. Apply a layer of uneven plaster to walls or color wash them with earthy colors to reproduce the texture of mud walls. Rub wax into flat paint or into wood to imitate the sheen of graphite clay pots.

This detail from a kitchen in southern Africa displays the most colorful end of the African spectrum. Black, purple, and bright green (all contained here in the dramatic painting) sit happily against the ocher red walls.

See also
Stone-ground,
Out of Africa,
Rural Retreat.

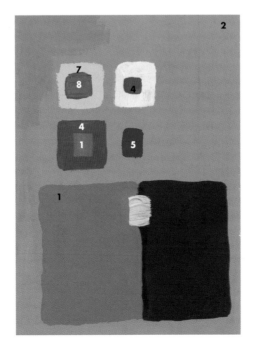

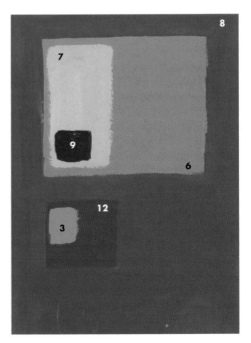

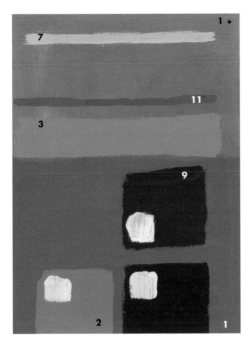

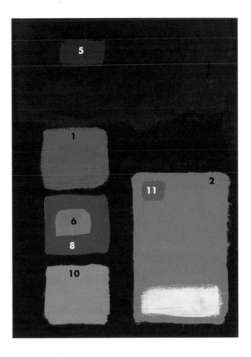

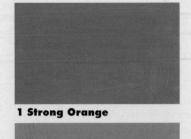

1 Strong Orange

2 Wet Clay

3 Clearwater Green

4 Ghana Red

5 Indigo Blue

6 Yellow Earth

95

African Visions

Although this interior is from a house in Andalucia in southern Spain, it has a strong African influence. The designer of the house was brought up in the Zambian bush. Baskets, clay pots, wood carvings, and bare wood furniture provide the finishing touches.

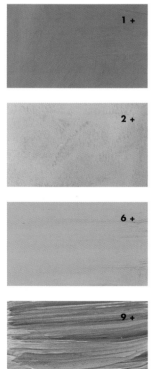

ADDING WHITE

Below you can see what colors 1, 2, 6 and 9 from the palettes look like when white is added to them.

1 +

2 +

6 +

9 +

7 Banana Yellow

8 Red Pot

9 Cocoa Bean

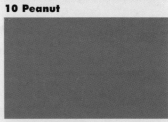

10 Peanut

11 Cloudy Blue

12 Palm Green

Rural Retreat

A casual country retreat is likely to have the same colors and finishes whether it is in New Mexico or Spain, Tuscany or the French Riviera. The old practice of lime washing results in an uneven paint texture, and colors like ocher and fresh blues and reds dominate. The colors are complex but not muddied, as they are often bleached or applied as thin washes and made from pigments. Use color washes and flat paint distressed to reveal a history of old colors. Few colors are used together and the contrast is kept to a minimum, so the effect is tranquil. This is light, lazy living, with few straight edges or neat corners. Terra-cotta tiles and pots are combined with simple fabrics in solid colors, stripes, and checks.

This detail of the staircase on page 100 shows the cloudy-blue lime wash complementing the old foxed etching.

See also
**Florentine Renaissance,
Stone-ground.**

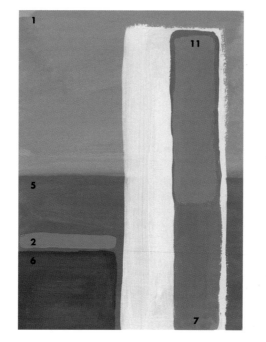

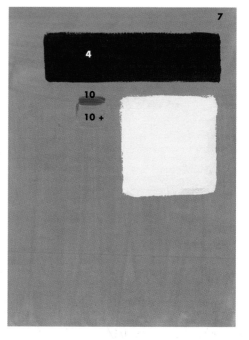

1 Eucalyptus Green

2 Desert Sand

3 Chestnut

4 Blue Gingham

5 Lake Blue

6 Forest Green

Rural Retreat

A staircase in an old French cottage has been lime washed and subsequently patched and repainted, resulting in a beautiful patina, suggesting many years' habitation and secrets. The gentle greenish-blues are reminiscent of Florentine colors, faded and softened.

ADDING WHITE

Below you can see what colors 5, 10 and 12 from the palettes look like when white is added to them.

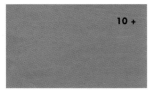

5 +

10 +

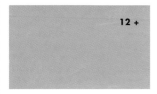

12 +

 complex colors

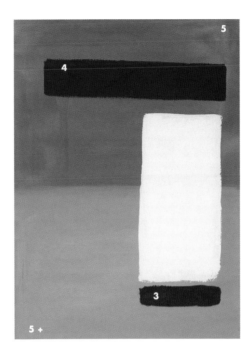

7 Mountain Blue

8 Red Earth

9 Spanish Pink

10 Suffolk Lime Wash

11 Lime-Washed Blue

12 Golden Sky

$\mathcal{E}$arly American

Simple and unpretentious, Early American is a mixture of folk and peasant styles that originally derived from all over Europe. Because the settlers had few resources, they made colors using plant dyes and easily available pigments, such as yellow ocher earth, brick dust, and lamp soot. Usually the colors were muted, with just a few used in a room. Apart from the ocher yellow and red, typical colors were smoky gray-blues, dusty rose pink, deep purplish-brown, and gray-green. Furniture, floors, woodwork, walls, and ceilings were all painted, with stencils providing a cheap way to imitate expensive textiles and carpets. Finishes were flat or semimatte. When walls are white, the style can seem stark because of the contrast between the white and the muted, tonally similar colors.

This muted plum and sage green are complex, mellow colors. Purple is often regarded as a modern synthetic color, but it is also a color from nature—slate and heather-covered hills, for example.

See also
Rural Retreat,
Northern Light.

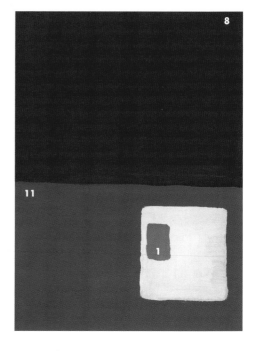

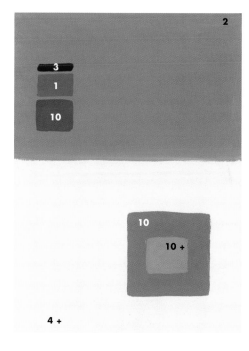

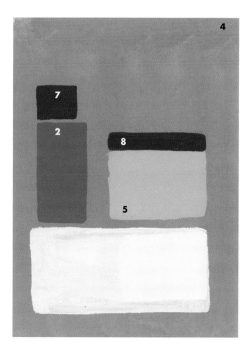

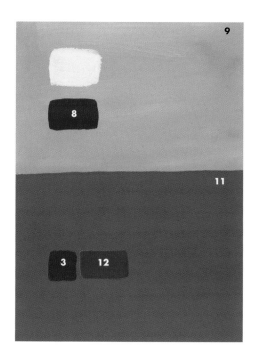

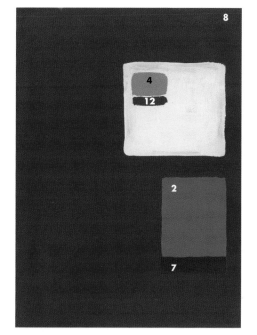

1 Dusty Green

2 Gray-Green

3 Brick Dust

4 Yellow Ocher

5 Pale Yellow

6 Teal Blue

Early American

Against an off-white background, the woodwork of this cottage has been painted with the uncluttered simplicity associated with Early American style. The strong contrast of the muted colors against the pale background is typical.

ADDING WHITE

Below you can see what colors 2, 4, 7, 8 and 10 from the palettes look like when white is added to them.

2 +

4 +

7 +

8 +

10 +

10

2 +

3

8 +

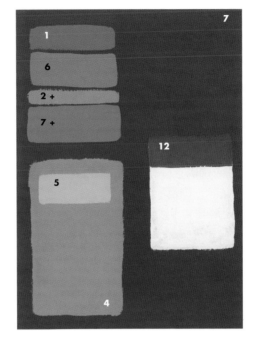

7

1

6

2 +

7 +

12

5

4

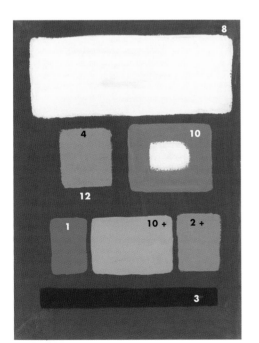

8

4

10

12

1

10 +

2 +

3

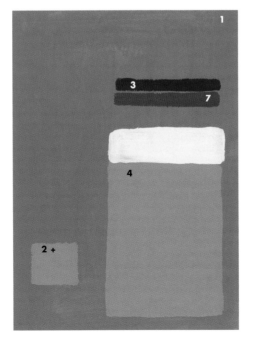

1

3

7

4

2 +

Early American

7–12

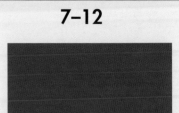

7 Dark Green

8 Barn Red

9 Williamsburg Gray

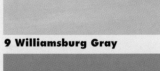

10 Grape Purple

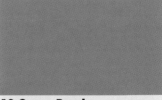

11 Cupboard Blue

12 Red Poppy

105

Utilitarian

The colors are based around a series of warm browns, using natural materials like wood and ceramics. These colors are brought out by the red lamps and contrasted with the olive green walls.

See also
**Chicago Deco,
Stone-ground.**

This is a style inspired by the 1940s—both its utilitarian aspect and the romance of the colonial look of the time, as seen in a Casablanca or Singapore clubhouse or bar, with its leather armchairs, rattan, and polished wood. Depending on the room in which it will be used, the look can be either dark or light, modern or nostalgic. The colors are complex secondaries and tertiaries that are slightly muted—deep lime green and tan with strong smoky blue, burnt orange, and garnet red. Grays and neutral beiges and creams are used in abundance. Because the palette is restrained, it relies on texture for definition, so fabrics should include leather, suede, and chenille. Exotic decorations—for example, mementos brought back from North Africa or the Far East—add a worldly, sophisticated element.

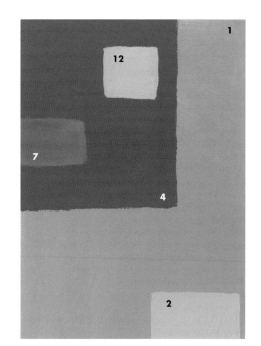

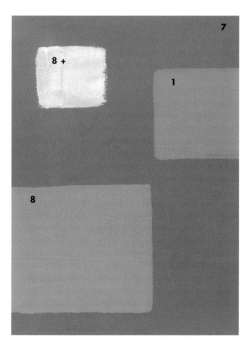

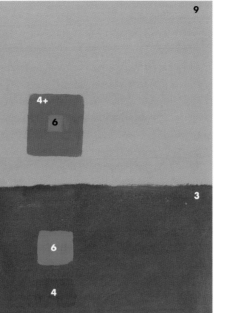

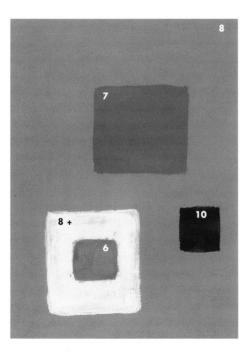

1 Lilac Blossom

2 Moleskin

3 Ginger Rust

4 Cocoa

5 Celadon Green

6 Lime-Peel Green

107

Utilitarian

Against a backdrop of olive green walls, the subtle colors and texture of the wooden floor and furniture, with the stone and brick fireplace, are brought to the fore. The period oak chairs give a dramatic sculptural quality to the otherwise minimally decorated room. Touches of ginger rust and pink also help to bring out the warmth of the wood.

ADDING WHITE

Below you can see what colors 4 and 8 from the palettes look like when white is added to them.

4 +

8 +

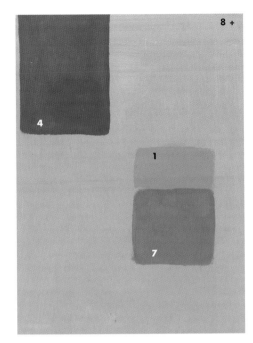

8 +

4

1

7

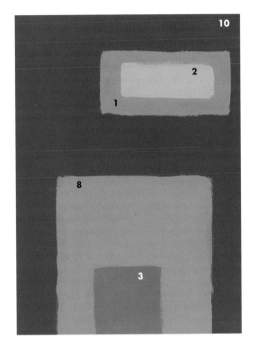

10

2

1

8

3

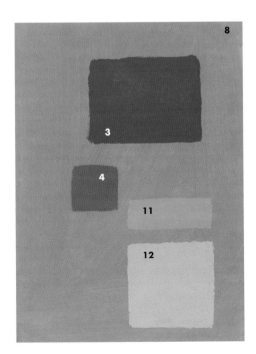

8

3

4

11

12

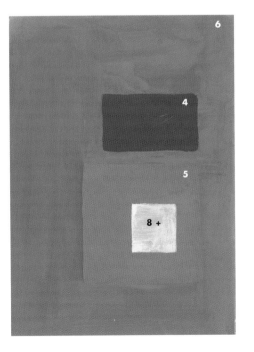

6

4

5

8 +

7 Olive Green

8 Cappuccino

9 Putty

10 Leather Brown

11 Bamboo

12 Chamois

Chicago Deco

The grayish aquamarine of these kitchen cabinets, combined with aluminum and wood, gives the room a distinctly 1930s look. The shiny black stove and retro teapot contributes to this effect.

ADDING WHITE

Below you can see what colors 4, 6, 7 and 10 from the palettes look like when white is added to them.

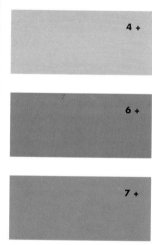

4 +

6 +

7 +

10 +

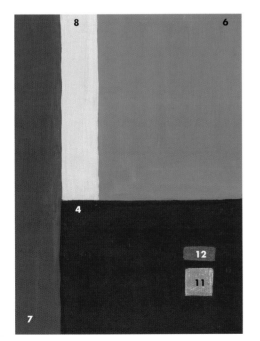

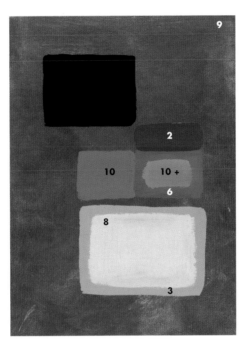

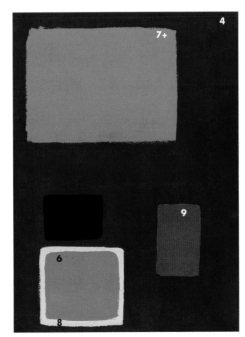

7 Grape Juice

8 Vanilla

9 Cherry Copper

10 Lake Gray

11 Silver

12 Gold

Northern Light

Scandinavian colors and decoration, particularly those of Sweden, came into their own in the eighteenth century when Gustav III was on the Swedish throne. Often called "Gustavian," the style derived from French and Italian neoclassical decoration, but the colors and interpretation are distinctively Swedish. Grayish blues and greens, combined with white, are the most common colors, and bring light into the interiors through the long, dark, Scandinavian winters. The tones are kept mellow and light, with ocher yellows and a dusty coral pink made from pale red oxide included for a little brightness. Few colors are used together and decoration is usually kept to a minimum. Combine these colors with bleached wooden floors, lightly painted furniture, solid and checked cottons, and woven fabrics to complete the look.

In this light and airy room, with its wooden walls painted in soft gray, a painted floor, and white curtains, the checked fabric of the chair throws provides the only hint of warm color.

See also
Early American,
Rococo,
Glam Diva.

2 +

11

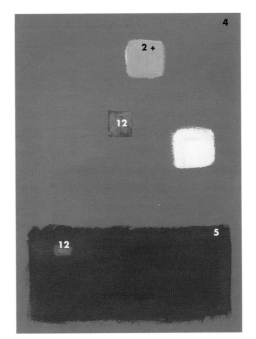

11

4

1 Dala Pink

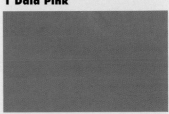

2 Gustavian Blue

3 Ocher Yellow

4 Nordic Gray

5 Oxide Red

6 Bright Verdigris

115

Northern Light

The soft blue-grays used in Swedish interiors are made inviting and welcoming because they are painted on wood, never given a shine, and are combined with soft and natural fabrics, such as linen and cotton. The ocher yellow in the chair fabric creates a sublime contrast with the walls and floor.

ADDING WHITE

Below you can see what colors 2, 3, 7 and 11 from the palettes look like when white is added to them.

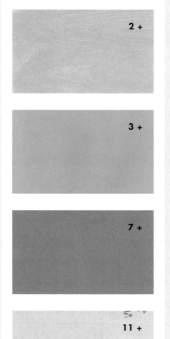

2 +

3 +

7 +

11 +

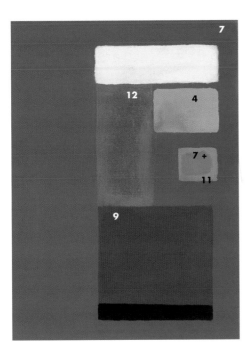

7

12

4

7 +

11

9

8

2

12

3 +

10

5
3

5

1

8

9

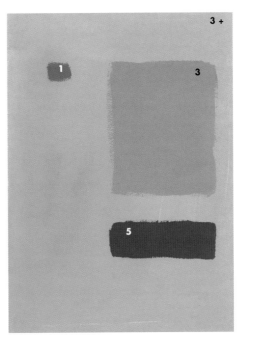

3 +

1

3

5

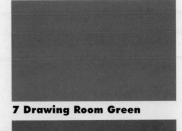

7 Drawing Room Green

8 Danish Blue

9 Lichen

10 Ivory

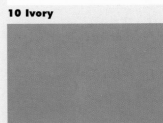

11 Gray Light

12 Gold

117

Elizabethan Pageant

At the court of Elizabeth I in sixteenth-century England, dark oak furniture, wainscoting, and tapestries provided a dramatic backdrop for fabulous fabrics and jewels. Used on bed hangings and upholstery, these included satins, damasks, silks, and lace, lavishly decorated with pearls and jewels. Embroidery such as crewelwork and stump work was decorated with golden threads and pearls. The colors included soft and subtle grays, lilacs, pale blues, pinks, and whites with red detailing. These pastel colors derived from natural dyes, so the colors were complex rather than simple and clean. Be inspired by this opulent style but try not to overdo it. Use embroidered and bejeweled pillows and fabrics from India, or decorate with subtle pastels contrasted with plaster white.

A detail from the picture on page 120 shows how a flash of bright red can enliven an otherwise muted interior.

See also
**Rococo,
Glam Diva,
Neoclassical.**

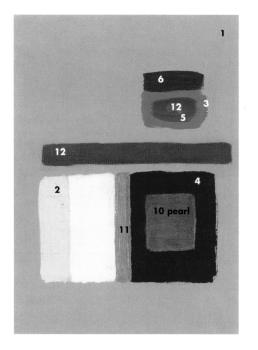

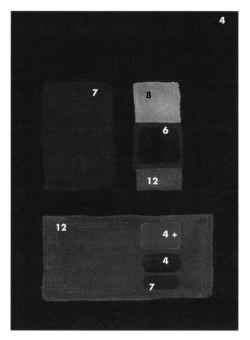

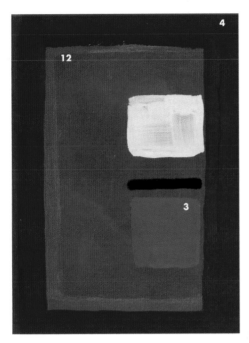

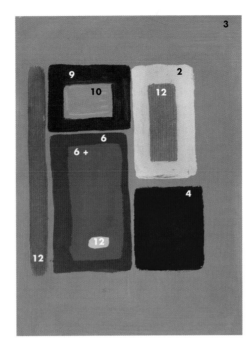

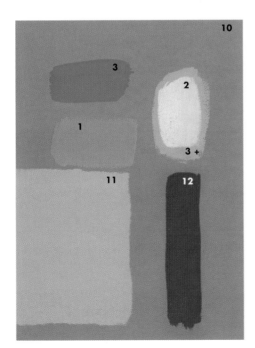

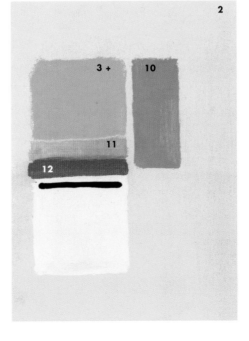

1 Cambridge Blue

2 Ivory

3 Midsummer Blue

4 Burgundy Red

5 Hilliard Blue

6 Field Green

Elizabethan Pageant

The strong pastel colors of this interior are reminiscent of a dress that Elizabeth I might have worn. The walls are colored unevenly and off-white is used on paintwork, while the decorative items are neutral-colored glassware and gold.

TEXTURE

A pearly sheen has been painted over color 10 to produce a delicate, shimmering lilac.

PEARL 10

ADDING WHITE

Below you can see what colors 3, 4, and 6 from the palettes look like when white is added to them.

3 +

4 +

6 +

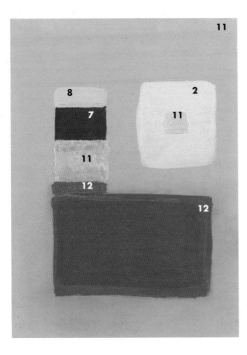

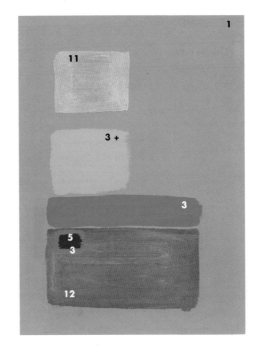

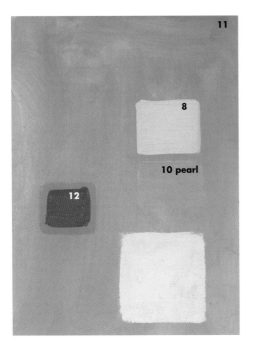

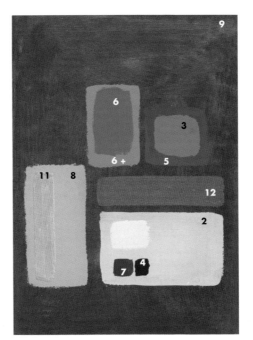

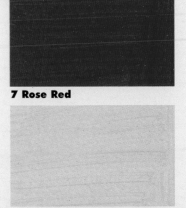

7 Rose Red

8 English Rose Pink

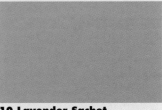

9 Mulberry

10 Lavender Sachet

11 Pearly Gray

12 Gold

Arts and Crafts

The Arts and Crafts movement swept through Europe and the United States during the late nineteenth century. The colors are predominantly cool, with blue and green often juxtaposed—a startling idea at the time. The palette in any one scheme is usually limited to just a few colors. Start with a soft white for walls or woodwork, and use a variety of olive greens, old gold and greenish lemon yellows, muted and lavender blues, and the occasional rich red and turquoise. The look is generally without strong contrast between the tones, and the finishes are matte. Natural fabrics like cotton and linen are the most appropriate. Furniture can be painted white, but waxed, unadorned oak is more rustic and authentic, and also provides a cool contrast.

The Arts and Crafts movement has influenced this kitchen and dining room, in both style and color. The sage green wainscot with its high shelf is characteristic of Arts and Crafts interiors, as is the use of copper light fixtures. Copper, pewter, and brass are all appropriate for light fixtures, fireplaces, mirror frames, and accessories.

See also
**Victorian Parlor,
Utilitarian.**

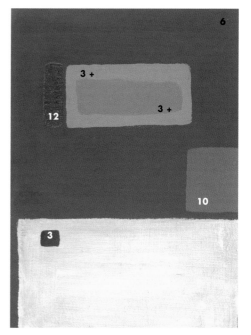

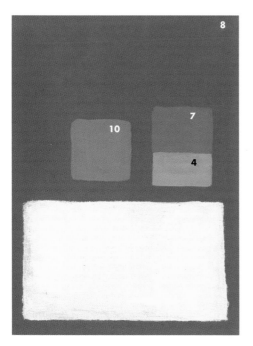

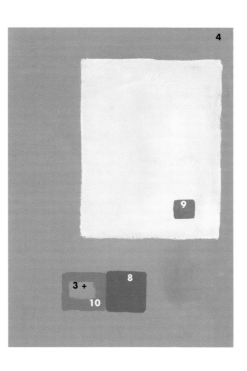

1 Pomegranate Pink

2 Oak Brown

3 Persian Blue

4 Greenery Yellowery

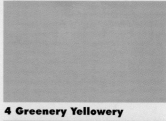

5 Damson

6 Majolica Green

Arts and Crafts

A large copper light hanging over the dining table picks up on its complementary—the pale blue of the door. In turn, the deep red of the far dining room wall enhances the copper fixture. Straw yellow walls in the kitchen act as a counterbalance to the cool blue door.

ADDING WHITE

Below you can see what colors 3 and 7 from the palettes look like when white is added to them.

3 +

7 +

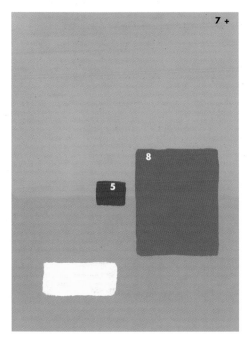

7 +

3 +

1

3 +

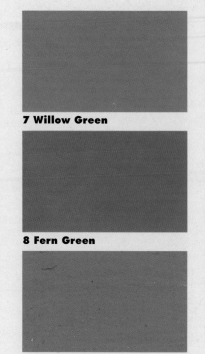

7 Willow Green

8 Fern Green

9 Peacock Blue

10 Pine-Needle Green

11 Terra-Cotta Copper

12 Gold

125

Florentine Renaissance

Anybody visiting Italy, especially Venice, Sienna, and Florence, cannot fail to be impressed by the beauty of the lime-washed walls of the buildings. This palette combines the earth pigments of red and yellow ocher with the sophisticated artist's colors found on Renaissance frescoes: cool, deep gray-blues, Bordeaux reds, deep greens, and olive greens. These stylish colors work in a rustic setting where the ochers are emphasized, but they can be used in a more opulent way reminiscent of a Renaissance palazzo. Use lots of colors together, maintaining a tonal harmony without jarring contrasts. A little off-white and cream need to be used to help show off the colors. The texture should be somewhere between the dead-flat finish of a fresco and the sheen of rich fabrics.

The interior of this Irish country house was designed and decorated circa 1870, as a tribute to Italy and the Renaissance. The ocher yellow walls and the colors in the della Robbia mantelpiece of glazed terra cotta all re-create the feel of the cinquecento.

See also
Rural Retreat,
Northern Light.

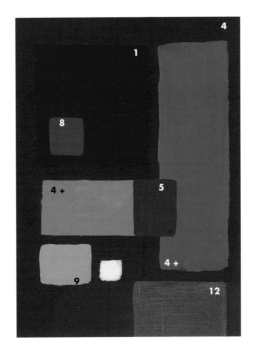
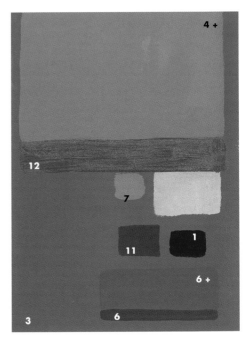

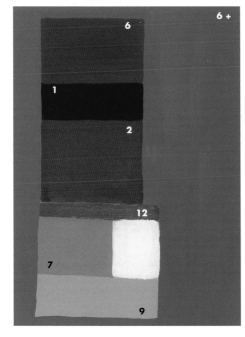

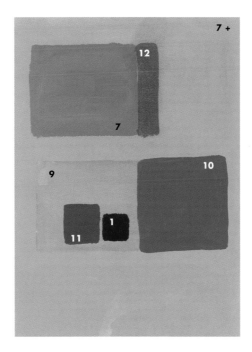

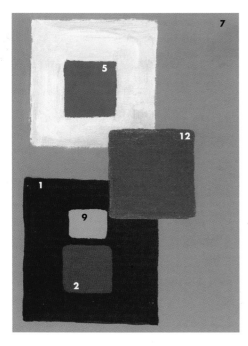

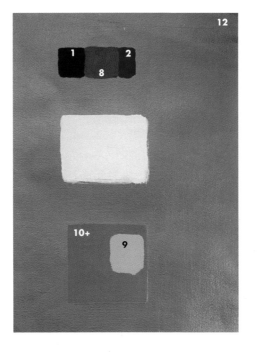

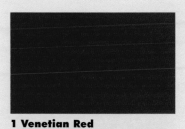

1 Venetian Red

2 Red Bole

3 Uffizi Gray

4 Bellini Blue

5 Madonna Blue

6 Majolica Green

Florentine Renaissance

Take inspiration from paintings of the
period and use the colors with
fabrics like brocade, silk, and velvet,
and, of course, with gold. A large
reproduction of a detail from a
Renaissance painting sets the scene
in this room. The greens and the
ocher pink used on the walls are
taken from the painting.

ADDING WHITE
Below you can see what colors 4, 6, 7,
8 and 10 from the palettes look like
when white is added to them.

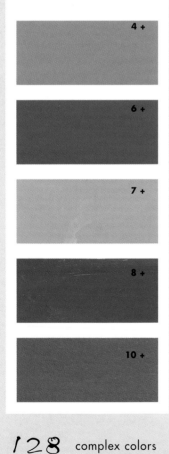

4 +

6 +

7 +

8 +

10 +

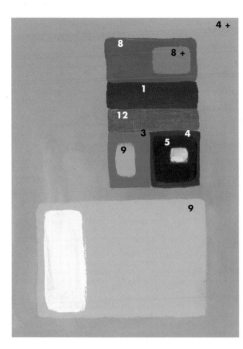

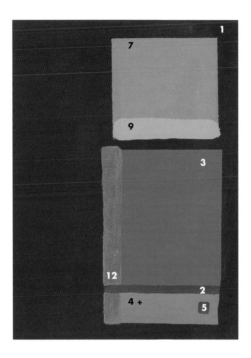

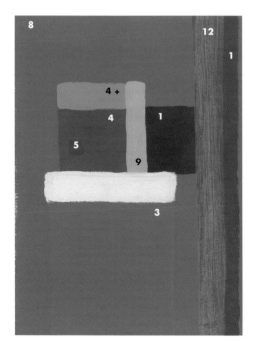

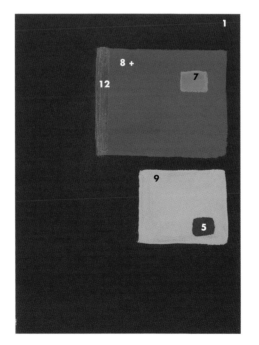

7 Italian Ocher

8 Medici Red

9 Old White

10 Brown Ocher

11 Terre Verte

12 Gold

Victorian Parlor

Highly developed and complex, the colors of the Victorian era were the result of nineteenth-century advances in synthetic-dye manufacture and mass production of printed fabrics and wallpaper. Almost no primaries were featured—instead, an abundance of strong but muted complex secondaries and tertiaries was used. A room might have contained a multitude of colors but the effect was not dazzling because they were similar in tone. Strong lavender, magenta, lilac, and heliotrope, as well as the colors of semiprecious stones such as amber and garnet, were extremely popular. This look is almost the antithesis of schemes using simple colors. Incorporate fabrics that have a sensuous feel, like velvet and chenille, and finishes with a slight sheen.

Using lilac as a wall color keeps the effect from becoming as overpowering as a traditional Victorian look. Gold and silver can be included, but instead of copper, use deep coppery gold.

See also
**Arts and Crafts,
Bohemian Rhapsody.**

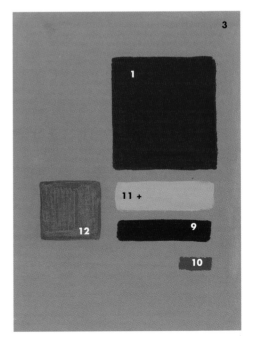

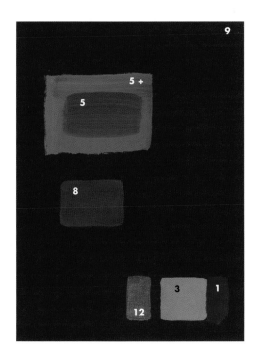

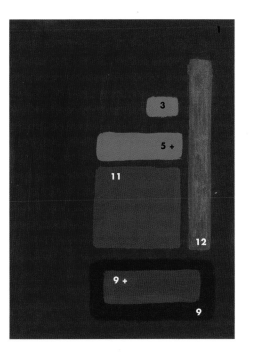

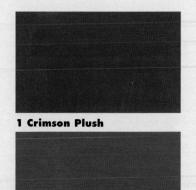

1 Crimson Plush

2 Madder Red

3 Golden Amber

4 Lavender Blue

5 Roman Purple

6 Moss Green

Victorian Parlor

This delightful room has been inspired by Victorian taste but has been given a modern update. Palms and Gothic Revival and Turkish Ottoman decorations echo the diverse sources of inspiration that were evident in nineteenth-century interiors.

ADDING WHITE

Below you can see what colors 2, 4, 5, 7, 9, 10 and 11 from the palettes look like when white is added to them.

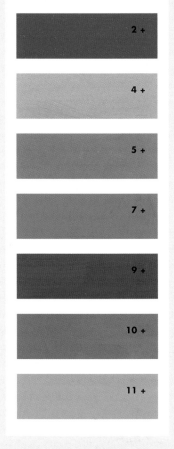

| 2 + |
| 4 + |
| 5 + |
| 7 + |
| 9 + |
| 10 + |
| 11 + |

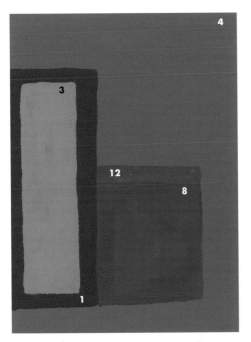

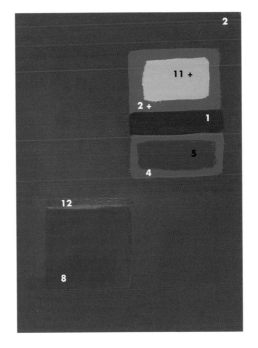

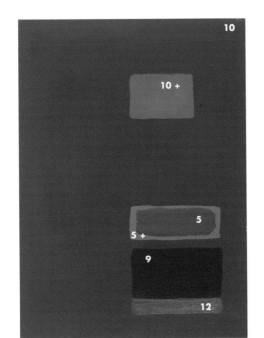

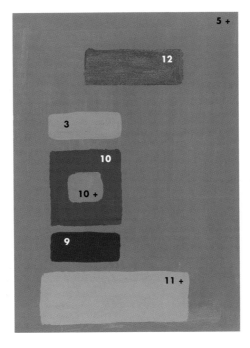

7 Olive Green

8 Bottle Green

9 Chocolate Brown

10 Meissen Blue

11 Taupe Brown

12 Copper Gold

133

Persian Palace

The colors of the Middle East are based around the cool tones of turquoise, aquamarine, and cobalt blue, with lots of white. Often a deep, rich red is included, as well as yellow ochers. The turquoise greens and blues are vivid but not sharp, so when you are mixing the paint, add a little terra cotta or orange to tone it down and a little white to keep it from looking harsh. Use only a few colors together, for example, crimson with ocher and turquoise. Crimson is often found as deep madder reds in carpets—the brighter the color, the less that is used. Persian or Turkish carpets obviously fit into this theme perfectly. Textures are usually matte, but accompanied by the shine of copper and old brass and the sheen of ceramics.

This room has been decorated with an eclectic mix of Middle-Eastern decoration, tiles, and painted furniture with European pieces. The soft aquamarine wall color provides a midtoned base against which are placed a range of tones, from the very dark furniture to the white bedspread.

See also
Hippie Chic,
Victorian Parlor.

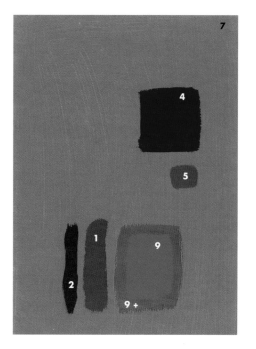

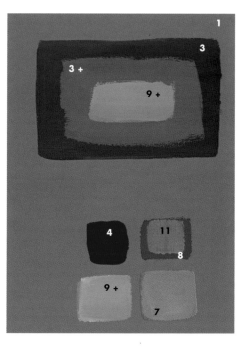

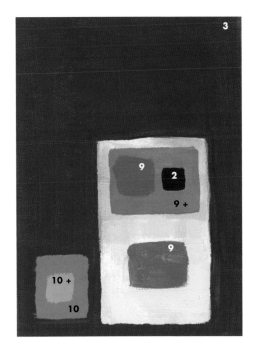

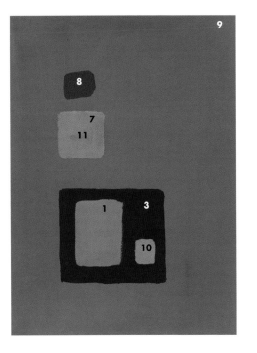

1 Turquoise Blue

2 Tile Blue

3 Ultramarine

4 Eggplant

5 Turkey Red

6 Emerald

135

Persian Palace

The wall color of this elegant bedroom is picked up by the stronger tones of turquoise, pink, and dark green in the curtains and tiles, while red and warm gold bring the whole room to life.

ADDING WHITE

Below you can see what colors 1, 3, 5, 9 and 10 from the palettes look like when white is added to them.

1 +

3 +

5 +

9 +

10 +

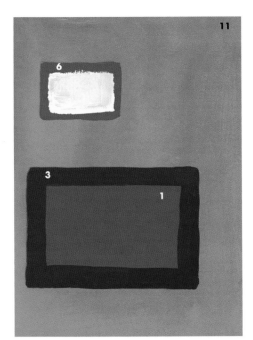

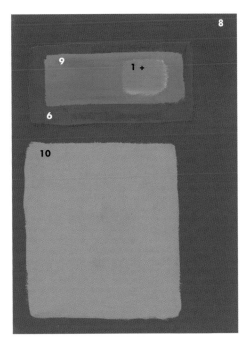

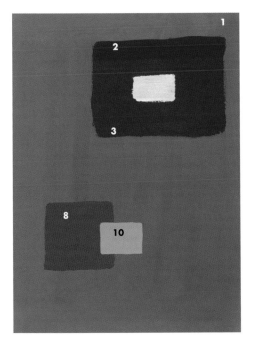

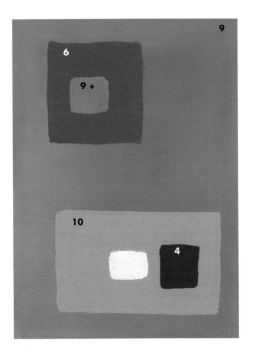

7 Amber

8 Nut Brown

9 Copper Green

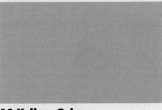

10 Yellow Ocher

11 Burnt Orange

137

Bohemian Rhapsody

You might find the color combinations of this theme in the homes of artists or designers, who are often daring in their use of color. The colors tend to be complex, but intense primaries and secondaries, as well as strong pastels, are also used. The emphasis is on mixtures in interesting, off-key combinations that almost clash—for example, bright pink and terra cotta or emerald and lime green. This uneasy association can make a room exciting and stimulating, if done skillfully. Colors are used in abundance, but careful matching of tone is important so that they do not counteract each other. Strongly colored pastels and neutrals are used to highlight and add dramatic tension. A mixture of textures and patterns may be used, typically with a flat or semimatte finish.

This Parisian interior incorporates color in a magnificent, offbeat way. Despite the use of a lot of colors, the room is not overwhelming because the greens, blues, reds, and purples are tonally the same. In the rest of the room, spots of strongly contrasting white and yellow, used with glass, mirrors, and crystal, keep it light.

See also
Ballet Russe,
Victorian Parlor.

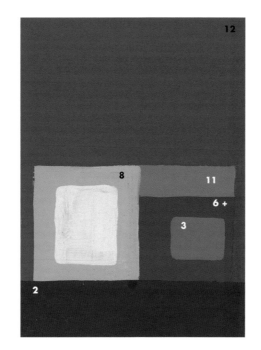

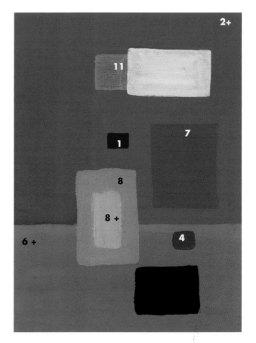

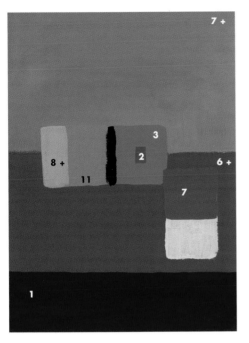

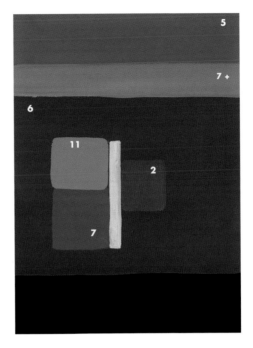

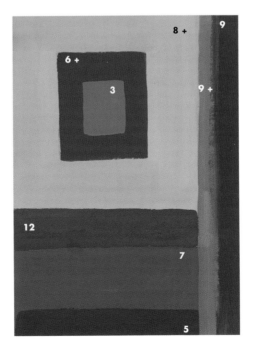

1 Leather Red

2 Viridiana

3 Brilliant Green

4 Poppy

5 Gainsborough Blue

6 Tyrian Purple

Bohemian Rhapsody

In this home in the Lake District, England, an old, gray leather chair provides a surprising contrast to a red-and-green painted wainscot and pink walls; these colors are also picked up in the carpets. Texture is a strong element in the room, from the shiny leather to the rough carpets.

ADDING WHITE

Below you can see what colors 2, 5, 6, 7, 8, 9 and 12 from the palettes look like when white is added to them.

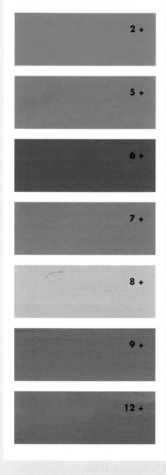

2 +

5 +

6 +

7 +

8 +

9 +

12 +

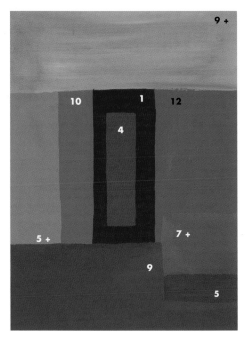

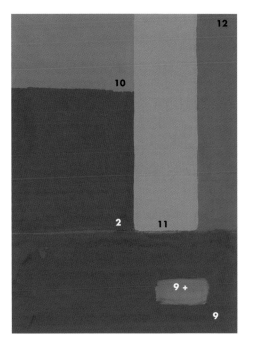

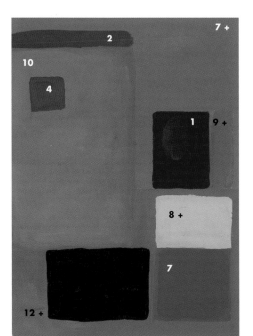

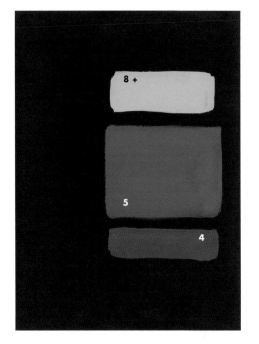

7 Pierro Blue

8 Charleston Yellow

9 Rust Red

10 Serge

11 Sienna

12 Serene Pink

Out of Africa

A style is emerging from different parts of Africa, encouraged by national pride. Based on traditional fabrics, the palette is a rich mixture of near-primary colors with some sharp and complex secondaries. Vivid maize yellow, dark pigeon-blood red, cerulean, forest green, and black are the staple colors. Magenta pinks and indigo blues are also used. As the colors are so strong and rich, no more than three or four colors are used together. Tonally, they are strongly contrasting. Yellow is often combined with black, green, or deep red. Paintwork finishes should be flat. The colors are found in fabrics like the traditional Ghanian kente cloth and East African kanga cloth, as well as batik and tie-dyed fabrics. Use these fabrics and colors with clay pots, baskets, and copper.

Africa has been brought to a Victorian house in London by using a mixture of fabrics and objects from all over the continent, including Egypt, Kenya, Mauritius, and Madagascar.

See also
African Visions,
Bohemian Rhapsody.

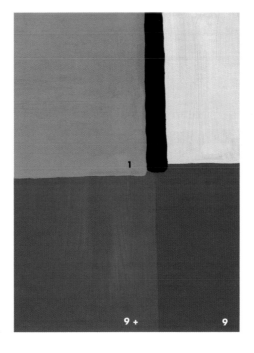

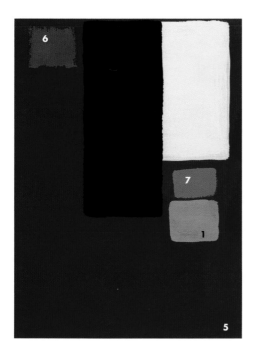

1 Maize Yellow

2 Indigo Blue

3 Madder Pink

4 African Green

5 Pigeon-Blood Red

6 Azure Blue

143

Out of Africa

The room has tremendous vibrancy because it is based on the electric combination of the complementaries purple and yellow. The mixture of patterns and colors, and the Islamic and tribal objects stimulate both the eyes and the head.

ADDING WHITE

Below you can see what colors 1, 2, 7, 9 and 10 from the palettes look like when white is added to them.

1 +

2 +

7 +

9 +

10 +

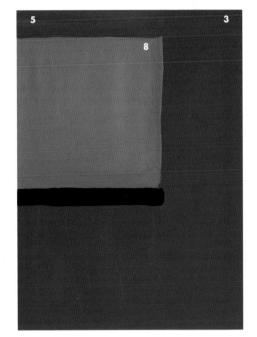

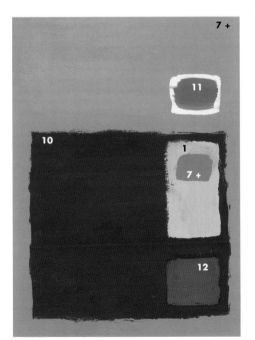

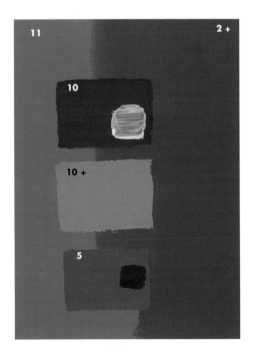

7 Turmeric Yellow

8 Sunrise Orange

9 Forest Green

10 Earth Brown

11 Dusty Blue

12 Flame Red

145

Hippie Chic

This theme brings together an array of colors, patterns, and fabrics from different cultures, particularly Moroccan and Indian. An abundance of offbeat colors is used, frequently in unusual combinations. Warm, slightly muted vibrant colors, such as indigo purples, dusky pinks, madder reds, and saffron yellow, are used in combination with kilims and other ethnic fabrics. These are unusual, nontraditional colors made from noncommercial, natural dyes. Keep the tones quite close, with one stunning, brightly colored or light area to bring the whole effect alive. Dulled gold or silver accessories work well, but nothing can be too jarring, as the general effect should be calming and even contemplative. Texture is important, so use soft, sensuous silks, crushed velvets, chenilles, and sheers.

This sitting room is alive with color, pattern, and texture, as if the souk had been brought inside. Using a strong, bright color on the walls allows you to use more muted colors and patterns.

See also
Persian Palace,
Victorian Parlor.

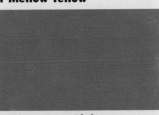

1 Mellow Yellow

2 Dusty Rose Pink

3 Purple Haze

4 Indigo Blue

5 Violets

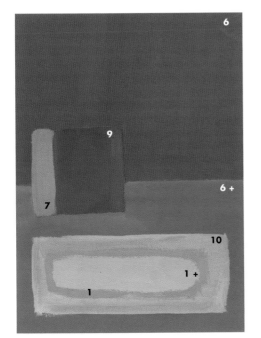

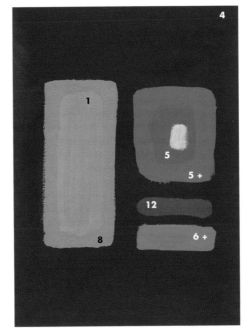

6 Copper Green

Hippie Chic

Despite the use of a lot of patterns and different objects, the room is bonded together by two main colors: hot saffron yellow and dusty pink. The remaining colors are generally cool.

ADDING WHITE

Below you can see what colors 1, 3, 5, 6, 8 and 11 from the palettes look like when white is added to them.

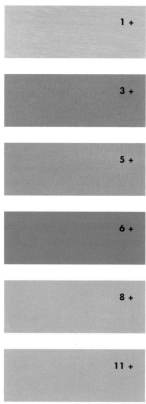

1 +

3 +

5 +

6 +

8 +

11 +

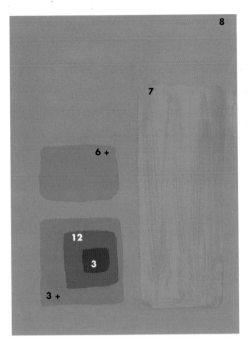

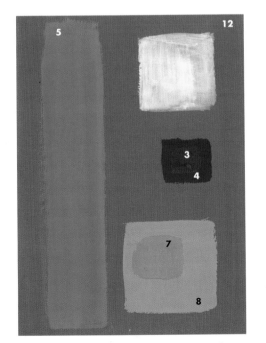

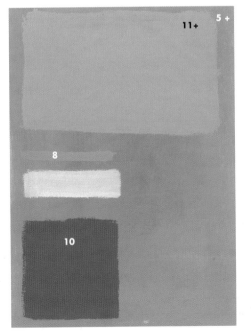

7 Tangier Orange

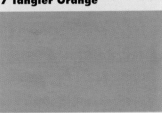

8 Spice Yellow

9 Burnt Earth

10 Moroccan Tile

11 Denim Blue

12 Strong Pink

149

Ballet Russe

Early in the twentieth century, the touring company Ballet Russe, under the direction of Sergei Diaghilev, brought Russian ballet to the West. The spectacular sets and flamboyant costumes, particularly those by Leon Bakst, revolutionized not just theater design but also fashion and decoration. The style is modeled after art nouveau, with its flamboyant, yet graceful lines, but it was also influenced by Japanese decoration, particularly kimonos and certain ceramics. Cyclamen, turquoise, violet, sharp lemon, lime, amber, dazzling orange, and peacock blue were used in vibrant and lively combinations, along with smoky blues and old pinks. Black was used extensively to emphasize the brightness of the colors, and by separating them, a large number can be used together.

Art nouveau and Japanese-inspired design are used alongside decorative items from the 1950s and modern pieces in this powerful room. The black brings all the colors together to create some very distinct tonal contrasts.

See also
Rock and Roll,
Simply Japanese,
Chinatown.

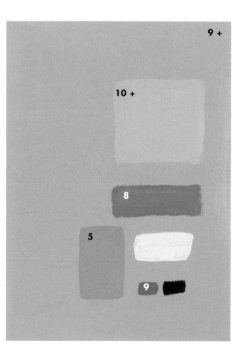

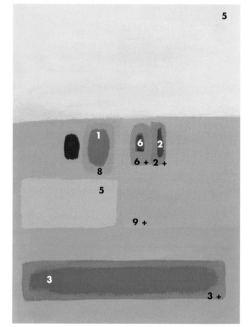

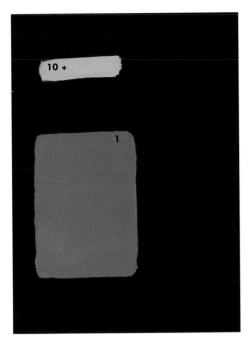

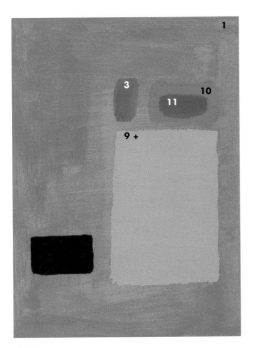

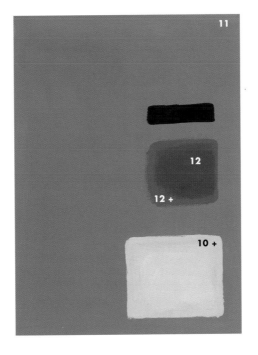

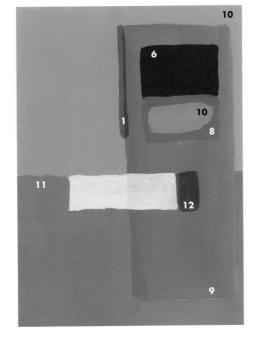

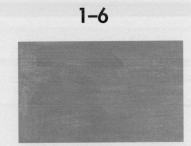

1 Clarice Orange

2 Scheherezade Purple

3 Poiret Pink

4 Erté Blue

5 Camisole Pink

6 Dark Viridian Green

Ballet Russe

Other designers of the 1920s and 1930s, such as the set and costume designer Erté, the fashion designer Paul Poiret, and the potter Clarice Cliff, also used black with radiant and dazzling colors.

ADDING WHITE

Below you can see what colors 2, 3, 6, 9, 10 and 12 from the palettes look like when white is added to them.

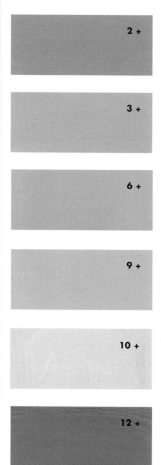

2 +

3 +

6 +

9 +

10 +

12 +

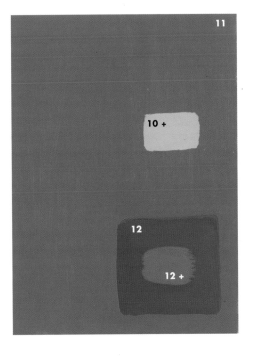

6 +
6
7
2 +
2
3
4
12 +
5
1

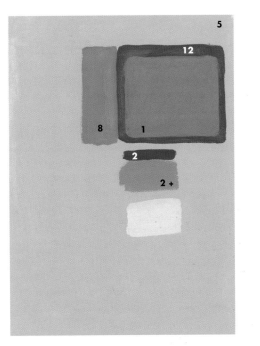

11
10 +
12
12 +

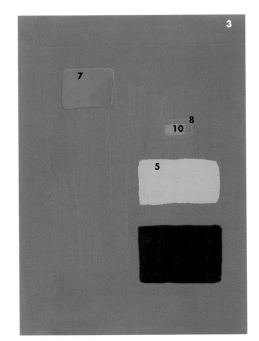

3
7
10 8
5

5
12
8
1
2
2 +

7 Peacock Blue

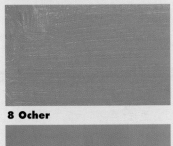

8 Ocher

9 Elephant Gray

10 Seaweed Green

11 Crocus Green

12 Cinnamon

153

The recipes

THE PAINT

Annie Sloan has used the widely available Kremer range of pigments to create the palettes for this book. The names of colors given in the recipes are the traditional names of the paint pigments. Newer versions of some of these pigments may be available under a variety of names created by the manufacturers or distributors. Therefore, Annie has used the traditional names of pigments as they have universal, recognizable standards. Where the amount of white is not specified in a recipe, it is up to the mixer to decide how much white to add to achieve the desired effect.

GOLD AND SILVER

A variety of golds, silvers, and coppers appear throughout the palettes. They are created using bronze powders. Below is a simple guide on how to achieve the right effect for your chosen color scheme.

- For traditional old gold, use warm gold-bronze powder.
- For modern gold, use green gold-bronze powder.
- For aluminum, use aluminum-bronze powder.
- For pewter, use dark aluminum-bronze powder.
- For copper, use copper-bronze powder.

BEACH HOUSE 30–33
1 **Yellow Sunshine** 1 part Cadmium Yellow, ½ part White
2 **Green Sea Foam** ½ part Viridian, ¼ part Raw Umber, White
3 **Sailor Blue** 1 part Cobalt Blue, ¼ part Burnt Umber, White
4 **Yellow Ocher** 1 part Raw Sienna, White
5 **Cool Bright Yellow** 1 part Lemon Cadmium Yellow, White
6 **Dark Blue Green** ¼ part Viridian Green, White
7 **Red Sails** 1 part Red Ocher, ½ part Vermilion, White
8 **Teal Blue** ½ part Cerulean Blue, ½ part Viridian Green
9 **Aquamarine Blue** 1 part Cerulean Blue, ¼ part Viridian Green, White
10 **Cerulean Sea Blue** 1 part Cerulean Blue, White
11 **Sea Moss Green** ½ part Cerulean Blue, 1 part Lemon Yellow
12 **Stainless Steel** 1 part Aluminum Powder

FLOWERY BOWER 34–37
1 **Old Rose Pink** 1 part Alizarin Crimson, ½ part Titanium White, ¼ part Yellow Ocher
2 **Mallow Pink** 1 part Alizarin Crimson, 1 part Titanium White
3 **Marigold** 1 part Earth Orange, 1 part Cadmium Yellow, White
4 **Lilac Blossom** 1 part Ultramarine Blue, ½ part Titanium White
5 **Poppy Red** 1 part Vermilion Red
6 **Cornflower Blue** 1 part Ultramarine Blue, ½ part Cerulean Blue, ½ part Titanium White
7 **Bay Leaf** 1 part Viridian Green, ½ part Raw Umber
8 **Sage Green** ½ part Cerulean Blue, 1 part Cadmium Lemon Yellow, 1 part Titanium White
9 **Apple Green** 1 part Cerulean Blue, 1 part Cadmium Lemon Yellow, ¼ part Titanium White

10 **Daffodil Yellow** 1 part Cadmium Yellow, White
11 **Autumn Tan** 1 part Red Ocher, ½ part Raw Sienna
12 **Dark Sand** 1 part Cadmium Yellow, ¼ part Yellow Ocher

MANHATTAN 38–41
1 **Lemon Mouse** 1 part Cadmium Lemon, 1 part White
2 **American Mustard** 1 part Yellow Ocher, ½ part White
3 **College Blue** 1 part Ultramarine Blue, White
4 **Navy Blue** 1 part Ultramarine Blue, ½ part Prussian Blue
5 **Clean Green** 1 part Cadmium Lemon, ½ part Prussian Blue
6 **Bottle Green** 1 part Viridian Green, ½ part Prussian Blue
7 **Cement Gray** ½ part Ultramarine Blue, ½ part Cadmium Orange, 1 part White
8 **Putty Gray** ½ part Raw Umber, ½ part White
9 **Strawberry** 1 part White, ¼ part Cadmium Red

10 **Redwood** 1 part Red Ocher
11 **Eggplant** 1 part Alizarin Crimson, ¼ part Burnt Umber
12 **Gold**

CANDY JAR 42–45
1 **Poster Blue** 1 part Ultramarine Blue, ¼ part White
2 **Turquoise** 1 part Cerulean Blue, ⅛ part White, ⅛ part Cadmium Lemon Yellow
3 **Orange Tangerine** 1 part Vermilion Red, 1 part Cadmium Yellow
4 **Poster Red** 1 part Vermilion Red
5 **Intense Pink** ½ part Ultraviolet Pink, ½ part White, ¼ part Alizarin Crimson
6 **Lemon Yellow** 1 part Cadmium Lemon, White
7 **Egg Yolk** 1 part Cadmium Yellow
8 **Emerald Green** 1 part Viridian Green, ¼ part Cerulean Blue
9 **Fluorescent Pink** 1 part Ultraviolet Pink
10 **Light Green** 1 part Lemon Yellow, ¼ part Viridian Green

11 **Deep Aqua**
1 part Cerulean Blue,
¼ part Viridian, White

ROCOCO 46–49
1 **Shell Pink** 2 parts White, 1 part Vermilion Red
2 **Terracotta Pink** 1 part Red Ocher, 1 part White
3 **Bordeaux Red** 1 part Alizarin Crimson
4 **Darkest Violet** 1 part Manganese Violet, White
5 **Prussian Blue** 1 part Prussian Blue
6 **Powder Blue** 1 part Ultramarine Blue, White
7 **Primrose Yellow** 1 part Cadmium Lemon Yellow, White
8 **Pale Golden Yellow** 1 part White, ¼ part Raw Umber
9 **Sage Green** 1 part Chrome Green, White
10 **Cool Umber** 1 part Raw Umber, 1 part White
11 **Gold**
12 **Silver**

ROCK AND ROLL 50–53
1 **Sharp Lemon** 1 part Yellow, ½ part White
2 **Orange Zing** 1 part Orange Vermilion, ½ part Cadmium Red, ½ part White
3 **Sputnik Red** 1 part Cadmium Red, ¼ part White
4 **Neon Blue** 1 part Cerulean Blue, 1 part White
5 **Baby Blue** 1 part Cobalt Blue, 1 part White
6 **Shocking Pink** 1 part Ultraviolet Pink, 1 part White
7 **Lime Green** 1 part Cadmium Lemon Yellow, ¼ part Prussian Blue
8 **Cement Gray** 1 part Ultramarine Blue, 1 part Red Ocher, 1 part White
9 **Platinum** 1 part Cadmium Yellow Dark, ½ Manganese Violet, 1 part White

10 **China Green** 1 part Green Earth, 1 part Cadmium Green, White
11 **Wisteria** 1 part Manganese Violet, White
12 **Cherry Red** 1 part Cadmium Red, 1 part Alizarin Crimson, ⅛ part White

IMPRESSIONISM 54–57
1 **Sunflower Yellow** 1 part Cadmium Yellow
2 **Citrus Yellow** 1 part Cadmium Lemon Yellow, 1 part White
3 **Tangerine** 1 part Orange Earth
4 **Terra Cotta** 1 part Burnt Sienna
5 **Paris Blue** 1 part Prussian Blue, ½ part White
6 **Ocher Yellow** 1 part Yellow Ocher
7 **Emerald Green** 1 part Viridian Green
8 **Purple** 1 part Manganese Violet, ⅛ part Burnt Sienna
9 **Picasso Pink** 1 part Red Ocher, ½ part White.
10 **Summer Green** 1 part Ultramarine Blue, 1 part Cadmium Lemon Yellow
11 **Matisse Blue** 1 part Ultramarine Blue, ¼ part Alizarin Crimson, ⅛ part White
12 **Claret Red** 1 part Vermilion, ½ part Alizarin Crimson

SIMPLY JAPANESE 58–61
1 **Cherry Blossom Pink** 1 part White, 1 part Vermilion, 1 part Burnt Umber, White
2 **Spice Red** 1 part Earth Orange, 1 part Red Ocher
3 **Lacquer Red** 1 part Cadmium Red
4 **Enamel Gray** 1 part Ivory Black, White
5 **Celadon Green** 1 part Earth Green, White

6 **Deep Violet** 1 part Manganese Violet, 1 part Burnt Sienna, White
7 **Peony Pink** 1 part Alizarin Crimson (Madder), White
8 **Cloisonné Green** 1 part Viridian Green, 1 part Prussian Blue
9 **Pebble Gray** 1 part Raw Umber, White
10 **Turquoise** 1 part Cerulean Blue, ¼ part Prussian Blue
11 **Charcoal** 1 part Ivory Black, White
12 **Gold**

BAUHAUS 62–65
1 **Clear Yellow** 1 part Cadmium Yellow Mid
2 **Pale Yellow** 1 part Cadmium Lemon Yellow, White
3 **Spectrum Red** 1 part Cadmium Red
4 **Plum Red** 1 part Alizarin Crimson, ½ part Burnt Umber
5 **Sand** 1 part Raw Sienna, ½ part Raw Umber, White
6 **Steel Gray** 1 part Lamp Black, White
7 **Klee Blue** 1 part Cerulean Blue, ¼ part Ultramarine Blue
8 **Nut Brown** 1 part Brown Ocher
9 **Ginger** 1 part Burnt Sienna, ½ part Vermilion
10 **Green Tea** 1 part Earth Green, ¼ part Yellow Ocher
11 **Burnt Orange** 1 part Earth Red, ¼ part Cadmium Red, White
12 **Aluminum**

PACIFIC ISLANDS 66–69
1 **Hibiscus Red** 1 part Cadmium Scarlet Red, ½ part Cadmium Lemon Yellow
2 **Frangipani Pink** 1 part Cadmium Scarlet Red, ¼ part Alizarin Crimson

3 **Coral Red** 1 part Vermilion, White
4 **Guava Orange** 1 part Cadmium Orange, 1 part Earth Orange
5 **Mango Yellow** 1 part Earth Orange, ¼ part Yellow Ocher, White
6 **Sunshine Yellow** 1 part Brilliant Yellow
7 **Banana Leaf Green** 1 part Cadmium Green, ⅛ part Cerulean Blue
8 **Island Green** 1 part Cadmium Green, 1 part Cerulean green
9 **Lagoon Blue** 1 part Cerulean Blue, ½ part Titanium White
10 **Gauguin Blue** 1 part Ultramarine Blue, White (for opacity)

CHINATOWN 70–73
1 **Emperor Red** 1 part Cadmium Red, ½ part Earth Orange, White.
2 **Gold**
3 **Ming Blue** 1 part Ultramarine Blue, White
4 **Cherry Blossom Pink** 1 part, Alizarin Crimson, ½ part White
5 **Bright China Blue** 1 part Cerulean Blue, ½ part White
6 **Imperial Yellow** 1 part strong Cadmium Yellow Mid, White (for opacity)
7 **Mandarin Orange** 1 part Earth Orange, ½ part Cadmium Yellow, White
8 **Dragon Green** 1 part Cerulean Blue, ½ part Cadmium Lemon Yellow, White
9 **Turquoise Blue** 1 part Cerulean Blue, 1 part Viridian Green, White
10 **Snap Dragon Pink** 1 part Rose Madder Hue, White
11 **Pale Yellow** 1 part Cadmium Yellow Mid, White

NEOCLASSICAL 74–77

1 **Lemon Yellow** 1 part Cadmium Lemon Yellow
2 **Empire Blue** 1 part Cobalt Blue, White
3 **Gentleman's Gray** 1 part Raw Umber, 1 part Brown Ocher, White
4 **Sandstone** 1 part Raw Sienna, White
5 **Gold**
6 **Lavender Blue** 1 part Ultramarine Violet, White
7 **Porcelain** 1 part Cerulean Blue, White
8 **Aubusson Pink** 1 part Indian Red, White
9 **Soldier Red** 1 part Cadmium Red dark, ⅛ part White
10 **Amethyst** 1 part Manganese Violet
11 **Forest Green** 1 part Prussian Blue, 1 part Cadmium Lemon Yellow
12 **Bordeaux Red** 1 part Alizarin Crimson

BOLLYWOOD 78–81

1 **Festival Pink** 1 part Ultraviolet Pink, ¼ part Alizarin Crimson, White
2 **Deep Cerise** 1 part Alizarin Crimson, 1 part Ultraviolet Pink
3 **Saffron Lemon** 1 part Cadmium Yellow Light, White
4 **Opal Green** 1 part Prussian Blue, ½ part Lemon Yellow, ½ part White
5 **Leaf Green** 1 part Cadmium Lemon Yellow, ¼ part Prussian Blue, White
6 **Orange Flame** 1 part Cadmium Yellow, ½ part Cadmium Red
7 **Temple Red** 1 part Cadmium Red dark
8 **Emerald Green** 1 part Viridian Green, 1 part Prussian Blue
9 **Hill Purple** 1 part

Ultramarine Violet
10 **Rajastan Blue** 1 part Ultramarine Blue, ¼ part White
11 **Silver**
12 **Gold**

GLAM DIVA 82–85

1 **Truffle Brown** 1 part Umber, ¼ part Alizarin Crimson
2 **Schiaparelli Pink** 1 part Ultraviolet Pink, White
3 **Lipstick Red** 1 part Cadmium Red, ¼ part Alizarin Crimson
4 **Dove Gray** ½ part Ultramarine Blue, 1 part Earth Orange, 1 part White
5 **Pansy Violet** 1 part Manganese Violet
6 **Black Currant** 1 part Manganese Violet, ¼ part Ultramarine Blue
7 **Buttercup Yellow** 1 part Cadmium Yellow Light, White
8 **Strong Aquamarine** 1 part Cerulean Blue, 1 part Viridian Green, White
9 **Sapphire Blue** 1 part Ultramarine Blue, 1 part Cobalt Blue, ¼ part White
10 **Mahogany Red** 1 part Burnt Umber, ½ part Alizarin Crimson, White
11 **Silver**
12 **Gold**

MAMBO CARNIVAL 86–89

1 **Hummingbird Purple** 1 part Ultramarine Violet
2 **Parrot Green** 1 part Viridian Green, ½ part Lemon Yellow
3 **Scarlet Red** 1 part Cadmium Red
4 **Hot Yellow** 1 part Cadmium Yellow, ⅛ part Vermilion
5 **Sunset Orange** 1 part Vermilion Orange
6 **Viridian Green** 1 part Viridian Green
7 **Mexican Blue** 1 part

Ultramarine Blue, ½ part Cerulean Blue, White
8 **Guatemalan Pink** 1 part Madder Red Hue, ⅛ part Ultramarine Blue, White
9 **Carnival Pink** 1 part Ultraviolet Pink, ½ part Madder Pink Hue, White
10 **Jungle Green** 1 part Prussian Blue, ½ part Lemon Yellow
11 **Electric Blue** 1 part Cerulean Blue Light
12 **Dusky Mauve** 1 part Ultramarine Purple, White

STONE-GROUND 90–93

1 **Slate** 1 part Ivory Black, White
2 **French Mustard** 1 part Raw Sienna
3 **Straw** 1 part Yellow Ocher, White
4 **Leather Brown** 1 part Burnt Umber
5 **Plaster Pink** 1 part Indian Red, 1 part Burnt Umber, White
6 **Brick Red** 1 part English Red
7 **Stone Gray** 1 part White, 1 part Raw Umber
8 **Fawn** 1 part Ocher, 1 part Raw Umber, White
9 **Blue Linen** 1 part Cobalt Blue, White
10 **Sky Blue** 1 part Cerulean Blue, ½ part Ultramarine Blue, ½ part Titanium White

AFRICAN VISIONS 94–97

1 **Strong Orange** 1 part Cadmium Orange
2 **Wet Clay** 1 part Burnt Umber, 1 part Raw Sienna, White
3 **Clearwater Green** 1 part Veridian, 1 part White, ¼ Prussian Blue,
4 **Ghana Red** 1 part Cadmium Red, 1 part Earth Orange
5 **Indigo Blue** 1 part Ultramarine Blue, 1 part Burnt Umber, White

6 **Yellow Earth** 1 part Yellow Ocher
7 **Banana Yellow** 1 part Cadmium Yellow, White
8 **Red Pot** 1 part Red Ocher, 1 part Earth Orange
9 **Cocoa Bean** 1 part Burnt Umber
10 **Peanut** 1 part Raw Sienna, White
11 **Cloudy Blue** 1 part Cerulean Blue, 1 part Burnt Umber, White
12 **Palm Green** 1 part Cerulean Blue, 1 part Lemon Yellow

RURAL RETREAT 98–101

1 **Eucalyptus Green** 1 part Chrome Green, ¼ part Viridian Green, ¼ part Raw Umber, White
2 **Desert Sand** 1 part Yellow Ocher, 1 part Cadmium Yellow
3 **Chestnut** 1 part Burnt Umber, 1 part Red Ocher, White
4 **Blue Gingham** 1 part Ultramarine Blue
5 **Lake Blue** 1 part Cobalt Blue, 1 part Viridian Blue, White
6 **Forest Green** 1 part Prussian Blue, 1 part Cadmium Lemon
7 **Mountain Blue** 1 part Chrome Green, ¼ part Prussian Blue, White
8 **Red Earth** 1 part Orange Earth, 1 part Burnt Umber
9 **Spanish Pink** 1 part Indian Red, White
10 **Suffolk Limewash** 1 part Vermilion, ½ part Red Ocher, White
11 **Limewashed Blue** 1 part Ultramarine Blue, ¼ part Raw Umber, White
12 **Golden Sky** 1 part Raw Sienna, 1 part Raw Umber, White

156 paint recipes

EARLY AMERICAN 102–105

1 **Dusty Green** 1 part Chrome Green, White
2 **Gray Green** 1 part Viridian Green, ½ part Raw Umber, White
3 **Brick Dust** 1 part Burnt Sienna, ¼ part Burnt Umber
4 **Yellow Ocher** 1 part Yellow Ocher, White
5 **Pale Yellow** 1 part White, 1 part Cadmium Yellow Mid
6 **Teal Blue** 1 part Prussian Blue, ¼ part Raw Umber, White
7 **Dark Green** 1 part Prussian Blue, 1 part Cadmium Lemon Yellow
8 **Barn Red** 1 part Alizarin Crimson, 1 part Red Ocher
9 **Williamsburg Gray** 1 part Ultramarine Violet, ½ part White, ½ part Yellow Ocher
10 **Grape Purple** 1 part Indian Red, 1 part White, ¼ Ultramarine Blue
11 **Cupboard Blue** 1 part Cobalt Blue, 1 part Burnt Umber, White
12 **Poppy Red** 1 part Cadmium Red

UTILITARIAN 106–109

1 **Lilac Blossom** 1 part Manganese Violet, White
2 **Moleskin** 1 part Burnt Umber, White
3 **Ginger Rust** 1 part Red Ocher
4 **Cocoa** 1 part Burnt Umber, ¼ part White
5 **Celadon Jade** 1 part Ultramarine Blue, ¼ part Raw Sienna, White
6 **Lime-Peel Green** 1 part Cadmium Lemon Yellow, ¼ part Black
7 **Olive Green** 1 part Cadmium Lemon Yellow, ½ part Earth Green

8 **Cappuccino** 1 part Burnt Umber, ½ part Yellow Ocher, White
9 **Putty** 1 part Raw Umber, ¼ part White
10 **Leather Brown** 1 part Burnt Umber, 1 part Red Ocher
11 **Bamboo** 1 part Yellow Ocher
12 **Chamois** 1 part Yellow Ocher, 1 part Cadmium Yellow, White

CHICAGO DECO 110–113

1 **Copper Green** 1 part Viridian or Phthalocyanine Green, White
2 **Bottle** 1 part Prussian Blue, 1 part Cadmium Lemon Yellow
3 **Gray** 1 part Ultramarine Blue, 1 part Burnt Sienna, White
4 **Eggplant** 1 part Alizarin Crimson, 1 part Burnt Umber
5 **Yellow Ocher** 1 part Yellow Ocher
6 **Eyyptian Azure** 1 part Viridian, 1 part Raw Umber, White
7 **Grape Juice** 1 part Manganese Violet, White
8 **Vanilla** 1 part Raw Umber, 1 part Burnt Umber, White
9 **Cherry Copper** 1 part Copper-Bronze powder
10 **Lake Gray** 1 part Cobalt Blue, 1 part Burnt Umber, White
11 **Silver**
12 **Gold**

NORTHERN LIGHT 114–117

1 **Dala Pink** 1 part Red Oxide (Red Ocher), White
2 **Gustavian Blue** 1 part Ultramarine Blue, 1 part Raw Umber, White
3 **Ocher Yellow** 1 part Yellow Ocher
4 **Nordic Gray** 1 part Prussian Blue, ¼ part Yellow Ocher, ⅛ part Red Ocher, White
5 **Oxide Red** 1 part Red

Oxide
6 **Bright Verdigris** 1 part Viridian Green, 1 part Raw Umber
7 **Drawing Room Green** 1 part Ultramarine Blue, 1 part Cadmium Lemon Yellow, White
8 **Danish Blue** 1 part Cerulean Blue, 1 part Raw Umber
9 **Lichen** 1 part Brunswick Green, 1 part Raw Umber
10 **Ivory** 1 part Yellow Ocher, 1 part Raw Umber
11 **Gray Light** 1 part Prussian Blue, ½ part Burnt Umber, White
12 **Gold**

ELIZABETHAN PAGEANT 118–121

1 **Cambridge Blue** 1 part Cerulean Blue, 1 part Cobalt Blue, White
2 **Ivory** 1 part Raw Sienna, 1 part Raw Umber
3 **Midsummer Blue** 1 part Cobalt Blue, White
4 **Burgundy Red** 1 part Madder Red Hue, ½ part Red Ocher
5 **Hilliard Blue** 1 part Cobalt Blue
6 **Field Green** 1 part Viridian Green, 1 part Cadmium Lemon Yellow
7 **Rose Red** 1 part Cadmium Red, ¼ part Alizarin Crimson
8 **English Rose Pink** 1 part Vermilion, White
9 **Mulberry** 1 part Prussian Blue, 1 part Raw Umber, White
10 **Lavender Sachet** 1 part Ultramarine Blue, 1 part Alizarin Crimson
11 **Pearly Gray** 1 part Ultramarine Blue, 1 part Raw Umber, White
12 **Gold**

ARTS AND CRAFTS 122–125

1 **Pomegranate Pink** 1 part Venetian Red, 1 part Earth Orange, White.
2 **Oak Brown** 1 part Brown Ocher, White
3 **Persian Blue** 1 part Cerulean Blue, 1 part Viridian Green, 1 part Raw Umber
4 **Greenery Yellowery** 1 part Cadmium Lemon Yellow, 1/4 part Black
5 **Damson** 1 part Alizarin Crimson, 1 part Burnt Sienna
6 **Majolica Green** 1 part Viridian Green, ¼ part Prussian Blue
7 **Willow Green** 1 part Green Earth, 1 part Cadmium Lemon Yellow, White
8 **Fern Green** 1 part Cobalt Blue, 1 part Cadmium Lemon Yellow, 1 part Raw Umber
9 **Peacock Blue** 1 part Viridian Green, 1 part Lemon Yellow
10 **Pine-Needle Green** 1 part Ultramarine Blue, 1 part Burnt Umber, White
11 **Terra-Cotta Copper**
12 **Gold**

FLORENTINE RENAISSANCE 126–129

1 **Venetian Red** 1 part Venetian Red, White
2 **Red Bole** 1 part Alizarin Crimson, 1 part Burnt Umber
3 **Uffizi Gray** 1 part Green Earth, 1 part Raw Umber, White
4 **Bellini Blue** 1 part Cerulean Blue, White
5 **Madonna Blue** 1 part Ultramarine Blue, White
6 **Majolica Green** 1 part Prussian Blue, 1 part Raw Sienna
7 **Italian Ocher** 1 part Italian Yellow Ocher, White
8 **Medici Red** 1 part Cadmium

Red, 1 part Alizarin Red

9 **Old White** 1 part Titanium White, 1 part Raw Umber

10 **Brown Ocher** 1 part Brown Ocher

11 **Terre Verte** 1 part Green Earth, 1 part Prussian Blue

12 **Gold**

VICTORIAN PARLOR 130–133

1 **Crimson Plush** 1 part Alizarin Crimson

2 **Madder Red** 1 part Madder Red Hue

3 **Golden Amber** 1 part Yellow Ocher

4 **Lavender Blue** 1 part Ultramarine Blue, 1 part Alizarin Crimson, White

5 **Roman Purple** 1 part Ultramarine Blue, 1 part Alizarin Crimson, White

6 **Moss Green** 1 part Brunswick Green, 1 part Cadmium Lemon Yellow

7 **Olive Green** 1 part Cadmium Lemon Yellow, ¼ part Black, White

8 **Bottle Green** 1 part Brunswick Green

9 **Chocolate Brown** 1 part Burnt Umber

10 **Meissen Blue** 1 part Cobalt Blue, White

11 **Taupe Brown** 1 part Burnt Umber, ½ part Ultramarine Violet

12 **Copper Gold**

PERSIAN PALACE 134–137

1 **Turquoise Blue** 1 part Viridian Green, ½ part Cobalt Blue, White

2 **Tile Blue** 1 part Cobalt Blue, 1 part White

3 **Ultramarine** 1 part Ultramarine Blue

4 **Eggplant** 1 part Alizarin Crimson, ¼ part Burnt Umber

5 **Turkey Red** 1 part Vermilion, ½ part Red Ocher

6 **Emerald** 1 part Cerulean Blue, 1 part Viridian Green, White

7 **Ottoman Sand** 1 part Raw Sienna, White

8 **Amber** 1 part French Raw Sienna

9 **Copper Green** 1 part Viridian Green

10 **Yellow Ocher** 1 part Yellow Ocher

11 **Burnt Orange** 1 part Earth Orange

BOHEMIAN RHAPSODY 138–141

1 **Leather Red** 1 part Alizarin Crimson, ½ part Burnt Umber

2 **Viridiana** 1 part Viridian Green, ¼ part Prussian Blue

3 **Brilliant Green** 1 part Cerulean Blue, ½ part Cadmium Lemon Yellow, White

4 **Poppy Red** 1 part Cadmium Red

5 **Gainsborough Blue** ½ part Prussian Blue, ½ part Cobalt, White

6 **Tyrian Purple** 1 part Manganese Violet, ½ part Ultramarine Blue

7 **Pierro Blue** 1 part Cobalt Blue, ⅛ part Burnt Sienna, White

8 **Charleston Yellow** 1 part Yellow Ocher, 1 part Cadmium Yellow, White

9 **Rust Red** 1 part Burnt Sienna, ½ part Vermilion

10 **Serge** ½ part Viridian Green, ½ part Raw Umber, White

11 **Sienna** 1 part Yellow Ocher

12 **Estate Green** 1 part Prussian Blue, ½ part Cadmium Lemon Yellow

OUT OF AFRICA 142–145

1 **Maize Yellow** 1 part Brilliant Yellow/Cadmium Yellow, 1 part Yellow Ocher, White

2 **Indigo Blue** 1 part Prussian Blue, 1 part Ultramarine Blue

3 **Madder Pink** 1 part Red Alizarin Crimson, 1 part Ultramarine, White

4 **Africa Green** 1 part Chrome Green, 1 part Cadmium Yellow, 1 part Raw Umber, White.

5 **Pigeon-Blood Red** 1 part Cadmium Red, 1 part Alizarin Crimson, 1 part Burnt Umber

6 **Azure Blue** 1 part Cerulean Blue, ¼ part Prussian Blue

7 **Turmeric Yellow** 1 part Raw Sienna, 1 part Red Ocher

8 **Sunrise Orange** 1 part Vermilion, 1 part Cadmium Yellow

9 **Forest Green** 1 part Prussian Blue, ¼ part Cadmium Yellow Lemon

10 **Earth Brown** 1 part Red Ocher, 1 part Earth Orange

11 **Dusty Blue** 1 part Cobalt Blue, ¼ part Burnt Umber, White

12 **Flame Red** 1 part Vermilion, ⅛ part Burnt Umber

HIPPIE CHIC 146–149

1 **Mellow Yellow** 1 part Cadmium Yellow, ¼ part Vermilion

2 **Dusty Rose Pink** 1 part Manganese Violet, 1 part Raw Sienna

3 **Purple Haze** 1 part Manganese Violet, 1 part Ultramarine Blue, White

4 **Indigo Blue** 1 part Prussian Blue, 1 part Alizarin Crimson

5 **Violets** 1 part Manganese Violet, White

6 **Copper Green** 1 part Viridian Green

7 **Tangier Orange** 1 part Vermilion, ½ part Cadmium Yellow

8 **Spice Yellow** 1 part Ocher Yellow, 1 part Raw Umber

9 **Burnt Earth** 1 part Orange Earth, 1 part Burnt Umber

10 **Moroccan Tile** 1 part Cobalt Blue, 1 part Raw Umber, White

11 **Denim Blue** 1 part Cobalt Blue

12 **Strong Pink** 1 part Ultraviolet Pink, 1 part Alizarin Crimson

BALLET RUSSE 150–153

1 **Clarice Orange** 1 part Vermilion, 1 part Cadmium Yellow

2 **Scheherezade Purple** 1 part Manganese Violet

3 **Poirot Pink** 1 part Ultraviolet Pink, 1 part Alizarin Crimson, White

4 **Erté Blue** 1 part Ultramarine Blue, ¼ part Prussian Blue

5 **Camisole Pink** 1 part Cadmium Red Dark, 1 part Burnt Sienna, White

6 **Dark Viridian Green** 1 part Viridian Green, White

7 **Peacock Blue** 1 part Cerulean Blue, 1 part Viridian Blue

8 **Ocher** 1 part Raw Sienna, White

9 **Elephant Gray** 1 part White, 1 part Manganese Violet, 1 part Yellow Ocher

10 **Seaweed Green** 1 part Cadmium Yellow, ¼ part Black

11 **Crocus Green** 1 part Prussian Blue, 1 part Lemon Yellow

12 **Cinnamon** 1 part Raw Sienna

Resource directory

Annie Sloan Practical Style
117 London Road
Oxford
OX3 9HZ
Tel (044) 01865 768666
Website www.anniesloan.com
(Kremer pigments, lusters and
bronze powders, wax, varnish,
brushes, paints, polished plaster, as
well as interior decorating problems)

Benjamin Moore & Co.
51 Chestnut Ridge Road
Montrale, NJ 07645
Tel (800) 344-0400
Website www.benjaminmoore.com

Best Liebco Corporation
1201 Jackson Street
Philadelphia
Pennsylvania 19148
Toll-free 1 (800) 523-9095
Fax (215) 463-0988
Email bestliebcp@aol.com

Dutch Boy
Website www.dutchboy.com
(Exterior and interior paints, tips
on painting)

Golden Artists Colors, Inc.
188 Bell Road
New Berlin, New York 13411-9527
Toll-free 1 (888) 397-2468
Tel (607) 847-6154
Fax (607) 847-6767
Email orderlineinfo@goldenpaints.com
Website www.goldenpaints.com

Grand Finishes
1541 Giammona Drive
Walnut Creek, CA 94546
Tel (925) 988 9990
Fax (925) 988 9991
(Paints, glazes as well as pigments,
waxes and specialty varnishes).

HK Holbein
Box 555, 20 Commerce Street
Williston, Vermont 05495
Toll-free 1 (800) 682-6686
Tel (802) 658-5589
Website www.holbeinhk.com

**Homestead House Authentic
Milk Paint**
95 Niagara Street
Toronto, Ontario M5V 1C3
Tel (416) 504 9984

Kama Pigments
85 Jean Talon Ouest, #4
Montreal
Quebec
Canada
H2R 2WB
Tel/fax 1 (514) 272-2173
Website www.kamapigment.com
(Retail, mail order and Internet
services in both French and English)

Kremer Pigments Inc.
228 Elizabeth Street
New York, NY 10012
Tel (800) 995 5501
Fax (212) 219 2395
E-mail kremerinc@aol.com
Website www.kremer-pigmente.com

**Painters and Decorating
Retailers Association**
403 Axminster Drive
St Louis, Missouri 63026-2941
Tel (636) 326-2636
Fax (636) 326-1823
Website www.pdra.org

Paint Effects
2426 Fillmore Street
San Francisco, California 94115
Tel (415) 292-7780
Fax (415) 292-7782
Website www.painteffects.com

Pearl Paints
308 Canal Street
New York, New York 10013
Toll-free 1(800) 221-6845 x2297
Tel (212) 431-7932 x2297
Website www.pearlpaint.com

Periwinkle Essential Stencils
P.O. Box 457
West Kennebunk, Maine 04094
Tel (207) 985-8020
Fax (207) 985-1601
E-mail periwinkle@cybertours.com
Website www.cybertours.com/
periwinkle/home.html

**Pierre Finkelstein Institute of
Decorative Painting, Inc.**
20 West 20th Street, Suite 1009
New York, New York 10011
Toll-free 1(888) 328-9278
Website www.pfinkelstein.com

R&F Handmade Paints, Inc.
110 Prince Street
Kingston, New York 12401
Toll-free 1 (800) 206-8088
Tel (914) 331-3112
Fax (914) 331-3242
E-mail mail@RFPaints.com
Website www.rfpaints.com

Sepp Leaf Products, Inc.
381 Park Avenue South
New York, New York 10016
Toll-free 1-800-971-7377
Tel (212) 683-2840
Fax (212) 725-0308
E-mail sales@seppleaf.com
Website www.seppleaf.com

**Sinopia Pigments &
Materials**
3385 22nd Street
San Francisco, CA 94110
Tel (415) 824-3180
Fax (415) 824-3280
E-mail pigments@sinopia.com
Website www.sinopia.com
(Pigments, traditional and modern
binders, gold and composition
leaf, decorative and lime paint.
Mail order.)

Stampers Studio
2255A Queen Street East
Toronto, Ontario
Tel (416) 690-4446
Fax (416) 690-7131
Website www.the-beaches.com/stampers

Index/Credits

PICTURE CREDITS

KEY: AvE = Andreas von Einsiedel; IA = The Interior Archive; EWA = Elizabeth Whiting & Associates a = above; c = centre; b = below; l = left; r = right; t = top

The publisher would like to thank the following for their kind permission to reproduce their photographs.
p 4 Red Cover: Andrew Twort; p 5 EWA:l; IA: Henry Wilson r; p 7 AvE: D Walter; p 8 Red Cover: Andreas von Einsiedel; p10 Collins & Brown; p 11 Ianthe Ruthven; p 12 IA: Ianthe Ruthven/Property: Knockalahara; p 13 EWA; pp 14/15 IA: Edina van der Wyck/Owner: Stewart; p 16 IA: Tim Beddow/Designer: Dido Farrell; p 17 IA: Inside Stock Image/G de Laubier; p 18 IA: Edina van der Wyck c; Henry Wilson/Designer: Philip Hooper cr; Henry Wilson/Antique Dealer: Peter Hinwood bc; Ianthe Ruthven: br; p 19 IA: Edina van der Wyck/Architect: Josh Schweitzer bl; Red Cover: Andreas von Einsiedel cl; Andrew Twort bc; EWA: c; p 20 IA: Fernando Bengoechea/Owner: Hunt Slonen bc; AvE: Timney Fowler cr; Red Cover: Andreas von Einsiedel c; EWA: br; p 21 IA: Henry Wilson /Designer: Brett Muldoon cl; Tim Beddow/Artist: Beazy Bailey c; Fritz von der Schulenburg/Title: Grace Woo Bruce/Private Hong Kong bl; Luke White/Owner: Renwick bc; p 22 AvE: Eliaschi bc; D Walter br; IA: Ianthe Ruthven/Property: Knockalahara cr; EWA: c; p23 IA: Tim Beddow/Property: Irish Cottage bl; Henry Wilson bc; Red Cover: Andrew Twort c; EWA: cl; p24 Red Cover: Andrew Twort c; Robert Harding Picture Library: Russell Sadur br; Lu Jeffery: cr, bc; p25 AvE: Timney Fowler cl; IA: Henry Wilson/Designer: David Hicks c; Lu Jeffery: bl; Tiggy Ruthven: bc; p26 AvE: r; Conway l; p 27 AvE: Eliaschi l; IA: Henry Wilson/Antique Dealer: Peter Hinwood r; pp 30, 32 IA: Edina van der Wyck/Architect: Josh Schweitzer; pp 34, 36 Ianthe Ruthven; pp 38, 40 AvE: Conway; pp 42, 44 Red Cover: Andrew Twort; pp 46, 48, 50, 52 EWA; pp 54, 56 IA: Tim Beddow/Property: Irish Cottage; pp 58, 60 AvE; pp 62, 64 EWA; pp 66, 68 AvE: D Walter; pp 70, 72 IA: Fritz von der Schulenburg/Title: Grace Woo Bruce/Private Hong Kong; p 74 IA: Henry Wilson/Designer: David Hicks; p 76 IA: Henry Wilson/Designer: Brett Muldoon; pp 78, 80 AvE: Eliaschi; pp 82, 84 IA: Luke White/Owner: Renwick; p 86 Red Cover: Brian Harrison; p 88 IA: Henry Wilson; pp 90, 92 Robert Harding Picture Library: Russell Sadur; p 94 IA: Tim Beddow/Artist: Beazy Bailey; p 96 IA: Tim Beddow/Artist: Rob Harding; pp 98, 100 Red Cover: Andreas von Einsiedel; pp 102, 104 Lu Jeffery; pp 106, 108 IA: Henry Wilson/Owner: Danielle Arnaud; pp 110, 112 Lu Jeffery; pp 114, 116 Tiggy Ruthven; pp 118, 120 Red Cover: Andreas von Einsiedel; pp 122, 124 IA: Henry Wilson / Designer: Philip Hooper; p 126 IA: Ianthe Ruthven/Title: The Irish Home/Castle Leslie; p 128 IA: Ianthe Ruthven/Property: Ballinterry House, Ireland; pp 130, 132 IA: Fernando Bengoechea/Owner: Hunt Slonen; pp 134, 136 IA: Henry Wilson/Antique Dealer: Peter Hinwood; p 138 Red Cover: Andreas von Einsiedel; p140 IA: Henry Wilson/Artist: Harrison; pp 142, 144 EWA; pp 146, 148 Red Cover: Andrew Twort; pp 150, 152 AvE: Timney Fowler.

Jacket:
Front IA Fritz von der Schulenburg / Title Grace Woo Bruce / Private Hong Kong r; Red Cover: Brian Harrison l; Back: Lu Jeffery.